Girls
with
Goals

clelia castro-malaspina

*To my soccer-loving siblings, Sebastian, Jean-Louis and
Claudia, and my soccer-tolerating brother, Fabrizio.*

*And to my former teammates who became lifelong friends:
Lauren, Caitlin, Erin, Alli and Blair.*

Girls with Goals © 2025 Quarto Publishing plc.
Text © 2025 Clelia Castro-Malaspina.

First published in 2025 by Holler, an imprint of The Quarto Group.
100 Cummings Center, Suite 265D, Beverly, MA 01915, USA.
T +1 978-282-9590
www.Quarto.com

ISBN 978-1-83600-189-8
EBook ISBN 978-1-83600-190-4

Cover photo credits (from top left, clockwise) © Bradley Collyer/PA Images/Alamy Stock Photo;
Paul Terry/Sportimage/Alamy Stock Photo; Bildbyran/Shutterstock;
Popperfoto/Getty Images; Francisco Seco/Associated Press/Alamy Stock Photo

Illustrations by Michelle Brackenborough

Designer: Michelle Brackenborough
In-house Design: Lyli Feng
Editor: Hollie Cayzer
Production Controller: Nikki Ingram
Art Director: Karissa Santos
Publisher: Debbie Foy

Manufactured in Guangdong, China TT012025

9 8 7 6 5 4 3 2 1

The paper and board used in this book are made from wood from responsible sources.

Photo: Mimi Snow

Clelia Castro-Malaspina is the author of books for teens and children, including *Your Freedom, Your Power: A Kid's Guide to the First Amendment*. She first played soccer when she was eight-years-old and has remained captivated by the sport ever since. Clelia has been an attorney and a literary agent, and currently runs her children's book editorial business, Mossy Pines Creative. She lives on Mercer Island, Washington, an island suburb of Seattle, with her husband and two daughters.

Contents

Introduction

On June 19, 1999, a major sports event was about to be held in East Rutherford, New Jersey. The thrumming crowds were headed to their seats, wearing their favorite athletes' jerseys, countless faces painted red, white, and blue, and the air dense with happy excitement. I know this because I was there. I was sixteen and I'd just finished my second year of high school. I'd been to Giants Stadium before to watch games, but this time was unlike any other. This time, among the fans, there were girls. Lots of them. Everywhere. And the athletes? They were all female. This was the opening match of the FIFA Women's World Cup.

Growing up as a kid who played and watched sports, I was a huge fan of the epic athletes of the 1990s. Michael Jordan, Wayne Gretzky, and Ken Griffey, Jr. were some of the super stars of American pro sports. And abroad, Brazil's Ronaldo, and France's legend, Zinedine Zidane were soccer icons—names even my American self knew well, thanks to my Peruvian dad and French mom. In the nineties, we didn't have social media influencers or hundreds of streaming shows to obsess over, so these larger-than-life athletes were some of our biggest entertainers and idols. All of these greats had something in common—they were all men. Growing up, I never expected to have a female sports hero. I never even questioned why there were hardly any. That was just the way it was, and the way it had always been.

Two years before the 1999 FIFA Women's World Cup, I had made my high school varsity soccer squad as a freshman—which, to me, was a huge deal. Days before high school had even started, my soccer team quickly became the most important thing in my life. My friendships with my teammates grew into best friendships, I looked up to the cool older girls, tried to impress my coaches, and whispered about the cute ones on the boys' team. I felt the pride of wearing my jersey to school on game days, the joy of getting out of school early for away matches, the heartbreak of losses, the thrill of winning, and the even bigger thrill of getting my name in the local paper because of a goal I scored. As a teenager, soccer was everything to me.

So when Mia Hamm and the rest of the U.S. women's national team emerged onto the scene, I was thunderstruck. For the first time in my life, I was admiring superstar athletes who wore sports bras and ponytails.

They were feminine—and also powerful and strong. And they were absolutely, epically awesome.

I was riveted when they won gold at the Atlanta Olympics in 1996, the first year the sport was at the Games. When I found out women had their own World Cup, and that some of the games would be played in my home state, you couldn't keep me (and tens of thousands of other girls and young women) away.

On that June day, not even a performance by one of my favorite boy bands, *NSYNC, could make me lose my focus on what I was there for: to see Mia Hamm, Brandi Chastain, Michelle Akers, Julie Foudy, Briana Scurry, and all the other incredible players in person. They beat Denmark in the first day of the tournament that would ultimately alter the course of women's sports history. It also altered something inside me. For the first time, I truly understood that women could be world-class athletes, capable of enthralling huge crowds—powerful, just like men. It was a big realization, and my friends and I were inspired. It made *us* feel powerful. We each assigned ourselves a member of the national team—I was the Julie Foudy. For the next month, I followed each game of the tournament, my entire enjoyment of the summer hanging on whether or not the U.S. won. My family was on vacation in Italy during the closing games of the tournament. Knowing how important the final match was, my parents had booked a hotel where we knew we could watch it live.

In the middle of the night, we gathered in front of a small TV and witnessed history.

I'd never been prouder to be a girl.

I'd also solidified my love of soccer—especially women's soccer—for the rest of my life.

Even at the time, that World Cup felt like the beginning of something. For so many years, I thought it had launched women's soccer to popularity. It wasn't until I was researching this book that I realized that the era of the 1999 tournament and those American players were far from the beginning of the story of women's soccer. So many heroines, struggles, victories, and amazing stories from across the world came before. The sport's success was built on almost 150 years of history.

Whether you're a fan or not, there is magic to the story of women's soccer. It's a story of constant obstacles, but also of constant persistence, incredible athleticism, and lots of triumph, all driven by a deep love of the world's beautiful game.

Clelia Castro-Malaspina

The author (No. 8), at age 16, posing with her high school soccer team in the fall of 1999, right after witnessing women's soccer history.

1

Kickoff

From very early on in human existence, where there was a ball, women and girls wanted to kick it. So did boys and men—but we all knew that already. Because women's history has often been poorly recorded, most people don't know that women and girls were there for soccer's beginnings too.

In a way, soccer sort of invented itself, evolving from one ball-based game to the next over time, until it finally morphed into modern soccer. Thanks to archaeologists, we know that human beings—even adults—have always had a deep-rooted need and love for play and creating games. Even early civilizations like the Maya, the Aztecs, and the Incans played games, including the first soccer-like games. The Aztecs called their sport *ollama* and played on a field called a *tlachti* that was shaped like the capital letter "I." The aim was to get a ball through a stone ring that was perched on top of a high wall using only your hips, knees, or elbows. This sounds fun—but it was apparently also very violent and bloody.

With a sport so deeply beloved, many cultures want to take credit for inventing the original form of soccer. There's the Romans who played *harpastum*, a game where players maintained possession of a ball. The Greeks who played a similar game called *epyskyros*. And there's the Egyptians who kicked around a ball made of wrapped

linens in celebration of the harvest. Most often, credit goes to the Chinese, whose game of *ts'u-chü* was probably the ancient root of modern soccer. The proof is in the name: "*ts'u*" means kick with a foot, while "*chü*" means a leather ball. First played around two thousand years ago during the Han dynasty, players tried to score goals using their feet and other body parts—no hands allowed. The biggest difference was that players looked up instead of out—*ts'u-chü*'s goal was thirty feet in the air.

Though these early forms of the game are from thousands of years ago, women weren't totally excluded. We know this because they appear playing in Egyptian hieroglyphs, Greek artifacts, and ancient Chinese artwork.

The idea that playing sports was absolutely inappropriate for women came later.

Writing the Rulebook

From its roots in *ts'u-chü*, soccer as we know it today emerged halfway across the world, in 1800s England. Soccer-like sports had been played in England by men for at least seven hundred years. By the 1800s, there were several different—yet similar—games involving balls and scoring goals. The rules differed depending on what school you went to, what city you lived in, or even what friend group you belonged to. Some groups allowed the use of hands, some didn't. Yet, all called the sport they were playing "football." Confusing! Sometimes teams, called football clubs, were formed with lots of excitement and anticipation, but when it came time to actually compete, the players couldn't because they had no one to play against—

no other club played the game with exactly the same rules! They were literally in a league of their own. "Football" in all its many forms at the time was very popular in England.

It wasn't until October 26, 1863 that eleven men from different football clubs, led by Ebenezer Cobb Morley, came together near London's Covent Garden to lay down official rules. Soccer as we know it was born. They formed the Football Association, a group that would govern the sport of football across England, and an organization that still stands today.

Getting in on the Game

So soccer was officially soccer. The rules were laid down and the players were all playing the same game. In England, men's club teams were flourishing, a league was formed and the concept of pro players emerged. Where were the ladies? Well, by the time modern-day soccer was invented, the general belief that sports weren't suitable for women had taken hold of society. It had become an established "fact" that women were more fragile and more delicate than men—that they were the "weaker" sex. What was the source of this harmful, sexist belief? It probably came from the fact that women get periods. Apparently, monthly bleeding was so alarming, it was a sign of fragility. There was also a theory floating around that all humans had a set amount of "vital force" in their lives, and any amount of exertion used up this vital force. When it was all used up, well, that was it for you and your existence. Between menstruating, carrying and bearing children, women had to use up a lot of the already "weak" vital force they had, so they couldn't waste any of it on sports. Better for them to stay home. For many centuries, this type of thinking was the rule, not the exception.

But, once again, where there was a ball, women and girls wanted to kick it. There's bits of evidence from things like old church registers, personal journals, and even poetry that women and girls played football—or a version of it—casually in those early years, among themselves or even with men. But as far as we know, it took nearly twenty years after the official establishment of soccer for women to formally get in on the game.

(Probably) the First Lady Footballers

On May 9, 1881, *The Glasgow Herald* of Scotland reported:

> ## LADIES' INTERNATIONAL MATCH
> ## SCOTLAND V ENGLAND
>
> A rather novel football match took place at Easter Road, Edinburgh on Saturday between teams of lady players.

It's believed that this is the first instance of a women's soccer match recorded by the press. As a result, this game that took place in Scotland goes down in history as the very first formally organized women's soccer game.

If the story of this first women's match was a Hollywood-produced movie, it would go something like this: a ragtag group of female athletes get together, bravely walk out of the shadows in their cleats, and show the world what they can do on the soccer field.

But, in real life, that's not quite what happened. The match was organized as a publicity stunt by someone the press mysteriously called an "Enterprising Advertising Agent." It highlighted an important rivalry between countries at the time, but whether the "Scotland" team was exclusively Scottish, and the "England" team completely English has been called into question.

First-Ever Ladies Line Up

Participants: 22 women   Ages: 18-24

Profile:
- Football fans who might have kicked a ball around as children
- Professional actors who wanted to "perform"
- Ladies with a spirit of adventure

Training period: two weeks

We don't know the exact identities of these first players because the team roster was filled with fake names. At the time, the very idea of women playing football was shocking and offensive to people who believed women belonged at home, not on the sports field—and there were plenty of those people. Hoping to avoid retaliation, the first female players had to hide who they really were. The pseudonym-filled rosters included Ethel Hay in goal, Belle Osborne in defense, and Minnie Brymner as forward for Scotland, while England had May Goodwin guarding the net, sisters Mabel and Maud Hopewell as the back line, and Geraldine Vintner up front. These ladies may have been too nervous to let people know their real names—but they weren't afraid to be the first women to officially step out and compete on the field.

It would be nice to say that this first women's game was treated like a true sporting event. But unfortunately, it wasn't—it was treated more like a spectacle, like the circus or a carnival show.

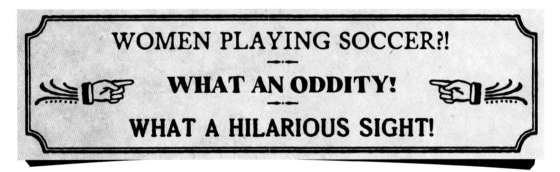

It was this sentiment that drew that first curious crowd.

Wearing blousy jerseys, billowy pants called knickerbockers, stockings, and high boots, the players took to the field and competed in front of an impressive crowd of 2,000. A player who went by Lily St. Clair scored the first goal—making her the very first woman to score a goal in a formal women's soccer match. In the end, Scotland bested England 3-0.

The reviews of the first game were not overflowing with compliments. One local paper reported that they were terrible—but *some* of the players weren't so bad. Not exactly high praise. The women weren't expecting much respect from the media anyway. They were doing something most considered totally inappropriate for women, after all.

Despite the lukewarm reception, the players considered that first match a success. People showed up (although about half the spectators left before the end), they received news coverage, and none of the players had faced bad consequences for playing. Best of all, they got to actually play this fun sport. Now it was time to take their ladies football show on the road! Matches were organized in various cities across England and Scotland. They played at local men's football clubs and advertised their games in local newspapers. The prospect of these additional matches must have been thrilling—they were going to get to play soccer again.

But after that first match, things took a turn. Many people—mostly men—showed up to watch them, but not so much as fans. They were there to gawk and heckle and yell obscene things. There seemed to be anger in the air among the male attendees over the fact that women were playing "their" sport. At two separate matches, rowdy spectators stormed the field.

That's right, the earliest female footballers were literally chased off the soccer field by men.

The first time, players were jostled and physically threatened before they fled the field with the help of the police and escaped in a horse-drawn bus. The second time, the players got wise. When the hooligans in the crowd looked like they were getting ready to breach the stands, the women ran off before they could get too close. In those first matches, it was downright dangerous to be a female soccer player.

The newspaper coverage of the matches also got uglier. Their level of play was not respected, with one journalist reporting that their training did nothing for them on the pitch. The reviews also cast doubt on the sport's appropriateness for women. One journalist called a match an "unseemly exhibition" and commented that the players' uniforms were "neither graceful nor becoming." Their femininity was also called into question. One paper referred to their competition as a "'ladies' football match." Putting quotation marks around the word "ladies" was a rude and sarcastic suggestion that these sports-playing women were not to be considered ladies.

The final match occurred in June 1881, less than two months after the tour had launched. In these first women's soccer matches, it seemed the level of play wasn't so great, the fandom was utterly menacing, and it was clear the public had a problem with women playing soccer. Even so, there was some magic there. It didn't really matter why some of these women chose to play—maybe some loved the game, but perhaps others were only there to create a spectacle or to make a statement about women's rights and abilities. But for the first time, women were able to get together and let loose on the field, kick a ball around, and compete to win a game—just like men. Imagine how utterly thrilling and freeing this must have felt for these women, who were expected to just stay at home all the time. And how it must have stirred something inside of those who played and those who witnessed or heard about these players. Press coverage of the games reached countries as far away as Australia and New Zealand—perhaps reaching the eyes of other female football fans who never dreamed an opportunity existed for them to play. Maybe these first games weren't perfect, but they were the beginning of something.

The beginning of something big.

Soccer Speak: Football or Soccer?

Many countries call the sport "football," while others call it "soccer." Who's right? If modern-day soccer really began in England, shouldn't we all just call it football? Well, it turns out that the English also invented the word "soccer." Students at the University of Oxford first used it in the 1880s to help distinguish the sports of rugby and what they called "association football," or "assoccer" for short—or "soccer" for even shorter. When soccer became popular in the U.S., "football" was already being used for another sport, so Americans decided on "soccer" instead. Soccer or football—same sport, different names. Many players and fans use the terms interchangeably, including the author in this book!

"Football" and "Soccer" aren't the only set of different terms that Brits and Americans use to describe the same thing. Here are a few other examples:

Field—Pitch ⚽ Cleats—Boots ⚽ Uniform—Kit
Team—Club ⚽ Tie—Draw ⚽ Shin guards—Shin pads

2

Game On:
Nettie Honeyball and the
British Ladies Football Club

To really get the ball rolling on women's soccer, the sport needed a gutsy and visionary leader, someone who was willing to stand up to the many, many people who believed women only belonged at home and say:

"We're doing this anyway!"

Thirteen years after those initial matches in England and Scotland, the world said hello to Nettie Honeyball, the Englishwoman who founded the British Ladies Football Club, the very first of its kind. It was 1894, and women's soccer officially had its inaugural leader.

With a name like Nettie Honeyball, she was either born to play this role, or more likely, she christened herself with a loud and proud pseudonym. It's pretty telling that she still felt she had to protect herself with a fake name. That's because in late nineteenth-century England, women had a raw deal. They were basically thought of as the property of men. In the eyes of society, their value was limited to taking care of the house, bearing children, and raising them. Women couldn't vote, didn't have the same access to education and professions as men, and couldn't own property. They barely had the ability to make decisions about their own bodies.

This photo of Nettie Honeyball in her football kit was printed in the newspaper, scandalizing many.

All of this had been terrible for women, but the tides were finally turning. In the United Kingdom and in other countries, movements toward equal rights for women had gained real momentum.

What Nettie was proposing to do was unheard of. Sure, a few years earlier some daring women had taken to the field and staged a few matches, but that had been mostly for show—this was a more serious athletic endeavor. Nettie was proposing that women regularly, competently, and enthusiastically play a sport in an organized club, just like men. And more than that—the creation of the British Ladies Football Club was a thunderous statement:

Women had the right to do what they wanted with their bodies.

And these women were choosing to play soccer. Just like suffragettes and feminists, Nettie and these early female footballers were standing up for women's rights.

Making Sports History

To pull this bold venture off, the shrewd Nettie put together a plan: first, she needed to sign up enough women to field two teams. Then, she needed a coach and a place to play. She got to work.

To recruit players, Nettie turned to the only method of reaching a wide audience at the time—the newspaper. She paid for an ad that called for female players, declaring that this "manly game could be womanly as well." Although some men made bogus applications to make fun of or try to blow up the effort, in the end, thirty brave women answered Nettie's call. They ranged from fourteen to twenty-eight years old; were mostly single; middle-class; were from in and around London; and most notably, had never, ever played real soccer before.

Consider the kinds of women who were brave enough to sign up for this radical and revolutionary club. The roster probably included some who kicked around a ball with their brothers in alleyways and some who had enviously watched men play football from the sidelines. It probably also included feminists who were eager to show the world that women had the right to do what they wanted, including things considered masculine. Some women were probably also there simply for adventure or the opportunity for some troublemaking. And others were likely there for a mix of all these reasons.

Together, these women made sports history.

In addition to the thirty players, twenty non-playing women also signed up to support the club. Among them was a genuine celebrity of the times, Lady Florence Dixie. Nettie—whose cleverness deserves another shout-out here—knew that they needed the support of a respected member of the aristocracy to help legitimize the club in the eyes of society.

Enter Lady Florence, who was a fascinating and epic woman in her own right. She was a well-traveled adventurer, who once voyaged to the Patagonia region of South America and brought home a jaguar cub (it later went on to live at the London Zoo).

Lady Florence Dixie's social status helped legitimize the British Ladies Football Club.

She was also a pioneering female journalist who ventured off to far-flung places like South Africa to report on war. A feminist, she recognized the British Ladies Football Club as an opportunity to boost women's rights. With Lady Florence now on board, Nettie bestowed her with the title of president, while naming herself secretary and captain.

The British Ladies Football Club was now ready to take on the haters.

Given that none of the ladies, including Nettie, had ever really played before, they needed a great coach to teach the basic skills of the game and to create a team strong enough to draw a paying crowd. Nettie engaged J.W. Julian, a well-known halfback who had played for the popular men's teams Royal Arsenal and Tottenham Hotspur. Just like Lady Florence, he was a respected name that lent some weight to the operation. With a full roster and a coach, Nettie secured a place to train, and the British Ladies Football Club was up and running.

Now that the sporting aspects of the club were taken care of, Nettie turned her attention to building up hype. The only way the club was going to be successful was if they could attract a lot of press and spectators.

Their first public match had to be big. Really big.

Nettie went back to the newspapers to publicize the match—a contest between "North" and "South" London. She didn't shy away from her feminist intentions.

> **I founded the association [to prove] to the world that women are not the 'ornamental' and 'useless' creatures men have pictured.**
>
> — Nettie Honeyball
> Founder of the British Ladies Football Club

In these interviews—all conducted by male journalists—Nettie found herself defending skepticism about the seriousness of their play, whether football was too dangerous and unrefined for women, if they would be deterred by weather or criticism, and whether their clothing was appropriate. But the unshakeable Nettie projected the club's strength, passion, and genuineness, only occasionally losing her cool. When one journalist heard that some of the players were married, he reacted in horror: "The husbands—what about them?!" To which Nettie spicily replied: "What have they got to do with it? Why shouldn't ladies play football as well as men?"

Lady Florence also spoke to the media on behalf of the club, fielding the public's burning questions about what the women would be wearing on the pitch—assuring them that there would be no "straitjacket attire" to get in the way of play.

Their sensational PR campaign drew a lot of attention. In the weeks leading up to the game, the British Ladies Football Club was a buzzy topic in the press. Some applauded the efforts of these "new women" but many expressed disapproval and doubts about the club, insisting that a woman's body was "physically incapable" of masculine sports. These big opinions reflected the big interest in these lady footballers.

It was clear the public's curiosity was piqued.

But would they show up to the first match?

On March 23, 1895, the British Ladies Football Club had its opening game at the Crouch End Athletic Ground in Hornsey, England. Nettie and Lady Florence's skills as hype women and PR masters had been super effective. People arrived on foot, by train, and by carriage to witness this extraordinary sporting event.

With the North team dressed in red and the South team dressed in blue, the lady footballers took to the field with 10,000 sets of curious eyeballs on them. The players had not been expecting a crowd so large. Nerves were high. How would all these people judge their athletic performances? How would all these people judge the way they were dressed?

THE
British Ladies' Football Club.

President—**LADY FLORENCE DIXIE.**

THE FIRST LADIES'
FOOTBALL MATCH
(NORTH V. SOUTH)

WILL BE PLAYED ON

Saturday, 23rd March, 1895,

UPON THE

CROUCH END ATHLETIC GROUND,
NIGHTINGALE LANE, HORNSEY.
KICK OFF 4.30.

The Ladies' Match will be preceeded by

CROUCH END v. 3rd GRENADIER GUARDS,
KICK OFF 3 O'CLOCK.

Admission (including both Matches) 1s.
Covered Stand, is. extra.

Frequent Trains from Moorgate Street, Broad Street, King's Cross, and intermediate stations to Hornsey.

Ladies desirous of joining the above Club should apply to Miss NETTIE J. HONEYBALL, "Ellesmere," 27, Weston Park, Crouch End, N.

Footballs by COOK.   Caps by A. E. RAISIN, of Stroud Green Road.

W. & W. J. Mizen. Printers, 13, Stroud Green Road. N.

Notable players included Nettie herself in midfield, a goalie who simply went by "Mrs. Graham," a tiny but skilled player named Miss Gilbert who was later nicknamed "Tommy" by the crowd, and a multiracial player named Emma Clarke. In the end, the North trounced the South, 7-1. Unlike the games played in 1881, the crowd appreciated what they saw, and at the end of the match, the ladies were cheered off the field.

For that first match, the quality of play wasn't great. Their knowledge of the rules left something to be desired—they didn't even change sides at halftime. This was the club's first real go at playing soccer, and as would be true of any beginner team—including a men's team—their performance wasn't top notch. The poor play was something journalists feasted on in their reviews of the game. One journalist reported: "A footballer requires speed, judgment, skill and pluck. Not one of these four qualities was apparent on Saturday."

But to the British Ladies Football Club, there was no such thing as bad publicity. They knew they'd improve with more training and more matches. The important thing was that tons of people showed up, and the women got to play real football. The success of this first match was enough to launch the club onto a tour of the country and even beyond. Nettie's big vision for the club was becoming fully realized.

Hall of Fame:
Emma Clarke

Emma Clarke was one of the original players of the British Ladies Football Club. She was multiracial and is remembered and honored by many as one of the first Black female footballers in England. Interestingly, however, some historians have traced her heritage back to Sri Lanka, and believe her to actually be of South Asian heritage. One of the harmful effects of women's history being poorly recorded is that we have limited information about important women like Emma. We do know that Emma was a woman of color, and a pioneer who paved the way for many.

Teams on Tour

In the first few months of the tour, the club embarked on a hectic schedule where the ladies traveled all around England, playing match after match, sometimes as "North vs. South" and other times as the "Reds vs. Blues." Every time, crowds of thousands showed up. Often, the spectators were friendly and gamely cheered on the ladies, but others preferred to heckle and berate them. A couple of matches even resembled the 1881 games by ending up in riots and with the players dashing away to escape.

On the road, the women dealt with all the things that traveling men's teams might: missed trains, inclement weather, rowdy crowds, finding themselves short on players, and sleeping, eating, and bathing in a new place every few days.

It's fun to think about this crew of women gallivanting around England, bonding and forming friendships through the rigors of being on the road, the joy of being free to play soccer, and the rivalry of competition. Not to mention the courage it took for all of them to defy society's expectations.

For a while, the future of women's soccer seemed bright. Not only was the British Ladies Football Club playing large crowds and attracting buzzworthy press, but there were also other signs of success. Crowds beyond England's borders were eager to see the club play, and the ladies traveled to Scotland, Wales and Ireland. The club also inspired new, rival clubs including a team founded by one of Nettie's originally recruited stars, Helen Matthews, who called her squad: Mrs. Graham's XI.

When they weren't playing matches within their own clubs or against other women's clubs, the female footballers played men's teams. The men's teams weren't the strongest around, but it didn't matter to the crowds—they ate up these men vs. women matchups. The female clubs even won several games, much to everyone's delight (except the male players).

The End of an Era

But a few years passed, and the varnish of novelty started to wear off. The crowds dwindled. Not only that, but women's soccer had a force acting against it. That force was England's Football Association (often referred to as the "FA"), the very same association that had established the rules of soccer in the first place and was the governing body of men's football in England. From the start, the Football Association had not liked what the British Ladies Football Club was up to. For its first game, Nettie had planned for the ladies to play at The Oval, a popular cricket and football venue—but the FA barred that from happening. No matter, Nettie pivoted and found a new field to play on.

Then the FA started blocking female clubs from more venues, and it became tricky to find men's clubs that were willing to support them and let them the space. This was annoying, but the ladies could deal with it. But then the FA did something major—in 1902, it banned its affiliated men's clubs from playing any games against women. This was the death knell for the British Ladies Football Club and England's other female football clubs. The women vs. men games were the games drawing the biggest crowds by this time, and without them, there wasn't enough money being made to support the tours anymore. Why would the FA do this? It boils down to the fact that it didn't like that female clubs were attracting big crowds—sometimes bigger crowds than its own men's clubs. The women's clubs weren't governed by the FA so the FA wasn't seeing any of the money from their matches. It also appeared that they simply didn't like the idea of women embracing "their" game.

Despite all the initial hype and success, the British Ladies Football Club fizzled out. Although it had a bit more staying power than the 1881 tour, it was ultimately another failed launch of women's soccer. But this failure had created more forward movement. After all, this era was a more legitimate and wholehearted effort to normalize women playing football, the level of play was better, the uniforms better suited for actually playing a sport, and the fans less hostile. By drawing thousands of spectators and earning major press (and international) coverage, these women exposed thousands around the world to the possibility of women's football, and some of whom would be the next generation to carry on Nettie Honeyball's vision. Most importantly, during a critical moment where women's rights were being evaluated, these pioneering athletes had made a bold statement: women could choose to use their bodies to play football, too.

So far, there had been two starts and stops.

When would women's soccer be here to stay?

● ● ●

Global Game: Chile

England wasn't the only country where women's soccer was heating up. Women all over the world were discovering the game. Press coverage about the British Ladies Football Club helped spread the word farther too. In Chile, the first women's football club was established in the city of Talca around 1900. There's also record of a charity match between a women's team and men's team in 1905.

3

Dick, Kerr
and the First Golden Age of Women's Soccer

*I*t was 1920 and the day after Christmas—Boxing Day. The Dick, Kerr squad jogged out of the players' tunnel onto Goodison Park's pitch in Liverpool, England. Their insides were fluttering with nerves and they were filled with that special adrenaline that comes from really, really wanting to win. They'd played lots of well-attended matches before—but this was unheard of. The stadium was absolutely brimming with more people than they'd ever seen in one place before. Every single available spot was taken. There were even people watching from the trees. An astounding 53,000 men, women, and children had gathered to watch them compete. One of the biggest sporting events of the year, they'd find out later that 14,000 more had been turned away because there was simply no room. At the moment, Dick, Kerr was the most popular team in all of England and was world-renowned for being utterly unbeatable. Hearing the extraordinary noise that 53,000 fans make, the players had never felt prouder. When the players first joined up, they never would have believed that this many people would show up to support a football match between teams made up entirely of women.

Fifty-three thousand fans cheering on lady footballers? How did the crowd transform from jeering and skeptical during the British Ladies Football Club era to adoring and enthusiastic in less than twenty-five years? As improbable as it may seem, in early twentieth century England, for a moment in time, women's soccer was the hottest ticket in town. That is, until it all came crashing down. Again.

Men at War, Women at Work

The story of the first golden age of women's soccer begins in 1914.

With two failed efforts at getting their own soccer going, it seemed that society wasn't ready for women to play what it wholeheartedly saw as a sport for men—and only men.

But sometimes perspectives are changed because they are forced to.

Sometimes something so big happens that the way people view the world is completely shaken up. In 1914, the world witnessed the launch of World War I, a.k.a. "the war to end all wars" or the Great War. It was the deadliest and most horrific war humanity had ever seen up until that point. The warring nations, many of which were countries in Europe, were sending droves of their young and able-bodied men to the frontlines. Back home, jobs were left behind that still had to be done. There was also new, additional work needed to help sustain the war effort. Who could fill the shoes of the enlisted and drafted men? The answer was obvious but also totally unconventional. The answer was women.

Before the war, certain jobs were deemed inappropriate for women—jobs that involved using heavy machinery, required physical labor, or had any element of danger. But now that the men were gone, factory owners and employers sang a different tune about "the weaker sex." They decided women were strong enough to take on this labor, and, actually, it was the patriotic thing to do. Despite the horrors happening at the frontlines and the anxiety and grief happening at home, this unprecedented moment in time presented an opportunity for women to show the world what they were really made of. This moment also allowed women to learn new, hard skills, earn higher pay (although not as high as their male counterparts), and to support their countries when they needed them most. For the first time ever, towns were filled with women plowing fields, working in coal mines, offices, in manufacturing jobs, and as mechanics, bus conductors, and railway workers.

A Factory of Footballers

The story of women's football continues back in England, where the factories were now filled with female employees. Many of them were teenagers and young women in their twenties. All had stepped up when the country needed a "hidden army" to go to work while the soldiers fought abroad. Factory owners were eager to keep output up—they wanted to keep their girls healthy, strong, and out of trouble. In peacetime, the working men liked to play football during lunch, on breaks, and even after work. It was decided this tradition should remain, and the factory girls were encouraged to kick about too. Intrigued, amused, excited, or simply looking for a diversion—many were game.

Most had never played before, so the remaining men taught them how. Soon, during every break and after work, the factory yards were filled with young female workers running around kicking balls. The women loved it, and before long—just like they had done with their male workers—the factories were forming their own teams.

One of these factories was Dick, Kerr and Company in the northern city of Preston. Originally a company that created equipment for trains and trams, after the outbreak of the war, it completely pivoted its manufacturing business to create ammunition and other war work. There was such an enormous need for ammunition, that many other factories made the same transition. Like these other factories, Dick, Kerr was filled with young women working manufacturing jobs, handling dangerous machinery, and even explosive material. These women became known as the "munitionettes."

In October 1917, in the Dick, Kerr factory yard, twenty-six-year-old munitionette, Grace Sibbert, was teasing some members of the men's football team. Once again, their performance had been less than spectacular at the most recent match.

"I bet even we could do better!"

she howled, referring to her and her female friends. Little did Grace know that this taunt would lead to the creation of one of the most famous and powerful teams in women's sports history. The guys challenged Grace and her friends to a game—men vs. women. With her husband away at war in France, Grace must have seen this as a real break from all the hard work and anxiety. The challenge was accepted, and a match arranged. A female team was fielded and outfitted with kits they inherited from the men's team. They proudly (and probably a little nervously) wore their dingy secondhand black-and-white striped uniforms, which included actual shorts. Although the result of this first match of the female Dick, Kerr squad has been lost to history, judging by what came after, it must have been a big success. At the end, Grace was hailed a hero for having the gumption to inspire all of this and was gifted the match ball. It was official—the Dick, Kerr women's football team was launched. It was not the first of its kind—other workplaces had started to form women's football teams—but it was to become the very best of its kind.

Shortly after, the Dick, Kerr factory was approached by a local hospital to see if its factory girls could help raise money for wounded soldiers over Christmas. The hospital suggested a nice charity concert—but the Dick, Kerr munitionettes had an even better idea: an awesome women's football match.

They jumped at the chance to play again.

Now that the Dick, Kerr factory was forming a competitive squad, getting a spot on the roster became the thing to do. Two hundred women tried out. In the end, eleven were chosen. Unfortunately, Grace wasn't among them because she got sick with tuberculosis. Her time as a footballer was disappointingly short, but she was able to make a great impact on sports history.

The match was scheduled for after dinner on Christmas Day. Their opponent would be the women's squad from the nearby Arundel Coulthard Foundry. The city of Preston was buzzing with anticipation. Excitement even filtered into the male ranks of the Dick, Kerr workers. One male employee of the company, a draftsman named Alfred Frankland, had always enjoyed watching the ladies play from his window overlooking the factory yard. He sensed that there was something special brewing here, and he wanted to be a part of it. He offered himself up to run the team as manager. With Al's help, Deepdale, the local men's football stadium, was secured for the match—a really big deal, as it was the home of a championship-winning men's football team. This was turning out to be a very serious affair.

For weeks, the newly minted Dick, Kerr team worked their hours at the factory, and off the clock, they prepared for the big game. They trained like a men's club, honing their skills with drills and building up their endurance with exercises like sprinting and skipping.

For the players, this was their rare chance to have some fun and to actually be an athlete. Before the war, no one had thought that women were strong enough to work hard manufacturing jobs, but they'd proven that wrong. Surely, they could play football too. And besides, the women were serving an even bigger purpose— this charity game was an opportunity to aid the war effort. The war had affected nearly every household, with many sons, brothers, and husbands killed or wounded. This was a way they could really help. Women weren't welcome on the battlefield, but they could raise money playing football to support their country.

The game was publicized through ads in the papers, posters, and plain old word-of-mouth. Without the benefit of pre-sales or RSVPs, the female squads had no idea what to expect on game day. Like their predecessors who faced so much criticism, they were going corset-free, playing "a man's game" by the same rules, and defying social expectations. But this time, like other female factory teams in England, they were raising money for wounded soldiers, a cause close to their community's and the whole country's hearts. Would people come to watch them play? Would the crowd be menacing or friendly? Would their weeks of training pay off? Did they have the skills to play like a real football team?

Just like the British Ladies Football Club's first match, this match drew a stunning 10,000 spectators. But this time, the crowd—while still curious and amused—was not mean-spirited. These girls were here to raise money for their boys at war, after all.

As the first all-female match in Preston started, the ladies got off to a wobbly start. The newspapers reported that, at first, they were giggly and awkward on the field—as if they were a bit embarrassed or shy. But after getting these nerves out, the girls accomplished what they set out to do—play a true game of football. That was the last of the giggles. The ladies sprinted hard, passed with precision, controlled the ball, made shots on goal and defended with heart. They showed off the skills they'd been honing in the factory yard and the strength and endurance they'd built from practices and working their physically-challenging jobs. The crowd cheered on both sides and seemed satisfied and even impressed with their level of play. In the end, Dick, Kerr got its first win of the multitudes to follow, beating the Coulthard's Ladies 4-0. Best of all, the lady footballers raised £600 for wounded soldiers, a large amount at the time. The girls were thrilled with the entire outcome.

Afterward, the newspaper coverage embraced the players' efforts. One local paper reported that the "quality of football show was much better than the [crowd] had expected." The same reporter called the performance "surprisingly good," some players "outstanding," that some put a "good deal of power into their kicks," and their shots on goal "were by no means to be despised." What a massive change in tone from twenty-five years earlier! The women were actually being reported on like the athletes that they were. Not like they were a garish spectacle or "freaks" to be mocked.

A Shift in Attitude

By the end of 1917, it seemed that women's football had truly taken off. Sure, there were still lots of naysayers and people who felt these women were acting too manly and didn't like that they were running around with their legs exposed. But overall, women's football was met with much more warmth than ever before. Why was it different this time around? Well, the exact circumstances of the era provided just the right recipe for this attitude shift. With most of the able-bodied men away at war, there were simply fewer opportunities to see football matches, and fans really missed going to them. Female footballers' skills had vastly improved during this era, and the games didn't feel like a downgrade. Watching women's football offered a joyful experience in a particularly gloomy era—something so many must have appreciated. And there was, of course, still the novelty of women playing football that drew a lot of curious spectators. What's more, because of the abundance of women now in the workplace, people's opinions had started changing about women's strength and physical capabilities. Seeing them as athletes just didn't seem so strange now that they did all of that hard, laborious work. Finally, and probably most critically, the women's matches were seen as patriotic because they raised money for good causes related to the war. A patriotic act was a socially acceptable act, and even more than that, a respectable and admirable act. All of these factors combined to make the setting just right for women's football to be accepted in a way it had never come close to before.

The Dick, Kerr squad was exceptionally good. Soon after that first match, they started traveling around, competing against the increasing number of squads sponsored by factories and other workplaces. Fan favorites emerged, like captain Alice Kell who led the fierce defense, and center forward Florrie Redford who had a special talent for scoring . . . and scoring . . . and scoring. Dick, Kerr just kept winning and raising more and more money for charities. Word spread about the unstoppable squad and thousands of fans showed up to every game. Charities realized if they recruited Dick, Kerr for a game, lots of money could be raised. And there were many charities in need, so the invitations kept rolling in, and there was no shortage of matches to play.

This was true even after a peace treaty was signed and the war officially ended in November 1918. The ladies were probably nervous about what the end of the war meant for them. With the return of the men, would things go back to what they were before the war? Would the women have to give up their jobs? Their football? Many women did have to give up their jobs, others chose to leave their jobs, but many remained in the workforce. In 1918, England granted women over thirty who owned property the right to vote—just a start in terms of equal rights, but a good sign that women had solidified their new position in society. In terms of football, the war had caused so much devastation and damage that charities still needed to raise a lot of money to help the many people in need. These female football games were a surefire way to fundraise. Because the matches were still considered patriotic and selfless in society's eyes, the women had earned the right to play on.

With all the press coverage and fanfare, the Dick, Kerr players had become national celebrities. Even so, they were still working-class women who had to make ends meet.

Imagine their days:

> ✔ *work long days at the factory doing hard, physical work*
> ✔ *train during breaks and days off*
> ✔ *play full, rigorous matches in front of thousands on the weekends (and sometimes on weeknights)*
> ✔ *travel to and from matches*
> ✔ *complete all the work that needs to be done at home*
> ✔ *do it all over again the next week*

It couldn't have been easy on their bodies, but being part of the team must have been so emotionally fulfilling for these women. They were connected not only because they trained and competed together, but because they were doing something extraordinary together—something no women had really been able to do before.

It was all worth it—even if they didn't make a dime for themselves. Although the players weren't paid their wages for the hours they missed traveling and playing, their wages were paid back by the money raised by ticket sales, with the rest going to charity. Financially, they broke even by being on the team. If the players were to actually earn money from these games, it would have been considered completely unseemly. Remember, one of the only reasons the public was tolerating this ladies-playing-football business was because it was only for charity.

These women did it all for a good cause—and for the love of the game.

Hall of Fame:
Lily Parr

To make the Dick, Kerr squad even stronger, manager Al Frankland started recruiting players from outside Preston. He would find out about a promising young player, locate them, get them a job at the factory or elsewhere in Preston, secure lodging, and then put them in a uniform. It wasn't that hard to do now that jobs for women were a bit scarcer and many female teams had been disbanded after the war. His greatest recruit—perhaps one of the greatest recruits in all of women's soccer history—was Lily Parr. Lily was the fourth of seven children who had grown up playing soccer in the streets of Preston with her brothers. She was a tall girl with a deep voice, known for her sharp sense of humor—and her wicked precision in passing and ability to nail a soccer ball right past any goalie. She quickly became the star player of this star squad. In 1920, during her very first season—at only fifteen years old—she scored forty-three goals. She would go on to score an astounding 850 more during her decades-long career with Dick, Kerr. Even today, she is known as one of the greatest players to ever play the women's game. With Lily as its superstar, the Dick, Kerr squad was on its way to becoming a worldwide sensation.

4

Going Global

Dick, Kerr continued its dominance and had beaten pretty much everyone around them, not only in England but in nearby Wales, Scotland, and Ireland. What was next for the unstoppable squad? Their eyes were set across the English Channel.

England wasn't the only country in the world experiencing the rise of women's soccer. In France, the women's rights movement had exploded, and alongside it, the development of women's sports. There had been a shift in thinking. The previous norm for female athleticism was limited to schoolgirls doing calisthenics—a type of strength training—to prepare them for future childbearing. But now, French women were taking part in real, competitive sports—like soccer. They didn't have factory clubs like in England, but they did have a few female athletics clubs. In 1919, the *Fédération des Sociétiés Françaises des Sports Féminins* (the Federation of French Women's Sports Clubs) was created with the help of Alice Milliat, an athlete who had a big vision for women's sports in France and beyond. She was a champion for women in sport and was willing to fight for their rights to play all sports, to have access to venues to compete in, for women's sports to be included in the Olympics, and for women to lead their own sports organizations and clubs. She was also president of the Paris-based female sports club, *Femina*.

Alice Milliat stands in a sea of men judging a long jump event at the 1922 Women's World Games, an event which led to the eventual inclusion of women's sports in the Olympics.

When Dick, Kerr approached her to ask if a French squad would come across the Channel and compete against them in four matches across England, the answer was a most definitive yes.

England Vs. France

These games were a huge deal. Other international matches had been played before, but those countries were part of the British Isles. This was France. Exotic, romantic, far-off France. It was also where many of England's men had been sent during the war to help defend it—and where many had died.

The countries were tied together in a tight bond.

When the French squad arrived in England, they were treated like royalty. Like Dick, Kerr, the team was mostly made up of working women—dressmakers, typists, machine workers, students. None of them had ever been to England before. They were welcomed to Preston with a brass band playing their national anthem,

The two team captains, Madeleine Bracquemond (left), and Alice Kell, shake hands at a training session before their match.

Dixième Année. — N° 359.
NOUVELLE SÉRIE : N° **18**.

Le Numéro : **50** Centimes.
ÉTRANGER : **60** Cent.

Jeudi **4 Novembre 1920.**

LE MIROIR
DES SPORTS

Abonnements :
1 An . . . 25 fr.
6 Mois . 13 fr.

Abonnements :
1 An . . . 25 fr.
6 Mois . 13 fr.

‖‖‖‖‖ PUBLICATION HEBDOMADAIRE ILLUSTRÉE, 18, RUE D'ENGHIEN, PARIS ‖‖‖‖‖

UNE JOUEUSE ANGLAISE, LYONS, SHOOTE AU COURS DU MATCH FÉMININ FRANCO-ANGLAIS DE FOOTBALL

La première partie de football, jouée en France entre deux équipes féminines anglaise et française, a eu lieu dimanche dernier au Stade Pershing et s'est terminée par un match nul : 1 but à 1. Elle fut disputée avec beaucoup d'entrain.

When Dick, Kerr came to France, the tournament was well-covered by the French media too. This shot of defending French footballers and Dick, Kerr's Minnie Lyons looking strong and athletic as she's about to boot the ball must have impressed—and shocked—many.

the Dick, Kerr ladies decked in new dresses they had sewed themselves, thousands of people and press lining the streets, and a big bouquet of flowers for France's manager, Alice Milliat. On their arrival, both teams were whisked away for dinner and a dance held in their honor.

These matches were largely seen as an act of goodwill. This French team traveled all the way to England to help raise money for British charities as a thank you to the soldiers who defended France during the war. The posters advertising the games read:

"THE FRENCH LADIES ARE PLAYING THE GAME HERE FOR THE LADS WHO PLAYED THE GAME OVER THERE!"

It was emotional, patriotic stuff, and emotions were running high. Public interest in these games was intense, and the press covered every step of the delightful tour, which made headlines across the world, exposing many to the idea of women playing soccer and even at the level of international competition.

When it came time to play, crowds of up to 25,000 showed up. Although the French team was quick and fit, their lack of experience showed and Dick, Kerr easily beat them in the first two matches. The French managed to tie Dick, Kerr in the next game, giving them the momentum to beat them in the last, which was held in London. Most of the women had never been to London before, and certainly had never stayed in such a luxurious place as the Bonnington Hotel. It was the experience of a lifetime. When it came time to say goodbye, the players hugged and vowed to stay in touch.

Of course, the French squad returned the invitation to compete on their home turf. And the Dick, Kerr ladies were thrilled to accept. The idea of this was absolutely wonderful—these working-class girls were going to Paris and would be treated like celebrities! In between state dinners, signing autographs, trips to iconic tourist sites like Versailles and the Eiffel Tower, and seeing with their very own eyes the devastation that war brought upon France, four games of football were played. France had been training hard since the first tour and it showed. They were able to tie the first match, but Dick, Kerr came roaring back with three wins.

These matches were covered widely in the media, and the female footballers' escapades reached countries beyond England and France—even as far as Australia and Brazil. All in all, these early international matches were about more than just football. They were about recovering from the emotional wounds of war, raising money for good causes, providing new perspectives for women who didn't usually get to see the world, and forming friendships between women who were connected by doing something extraordinary. Could it get better than this?

It could. After the celebrated France games, Dick, Kerr was more popular than ever. At one point, manager Al Frankland reported he had to turn down 120 different offers to play charity matches. The team's matches warranted souvenir programs, postcards and collectible cards bearing their photos, and a fictionalized series inspired by them published in a weekly magazine—an early form of fan fiction. The factory had even bought its own park that featured a real pitch for them to train on. When the 1920 Boxing Day match against St. Helens Ladies came, with a record-breaking crowd of 53,000 in attendance, Dick, Kerr won yet again. The team—and the sport of women's football—was on top of the world. How far they had all risen in just a few decades. But what the players didn't realize at the time was that it was their extraordinary success that would ultimately lead to their downfall.

The End of (Another) Era

The success of Dick, Kerr and women's football in England didn't sit well with everyone. Although many were on board with the new status of women's football, there was one group that very much was not, and that was England's Football Association. Again. Since it had first laid down the rules of modern football back in 1863, men's professional football had continued to develop, even though it was forced to pause during the war. The FA didn't have anything to do with the women's game—it didn't want to. Back in Nettie Honeyball's day, the FA had made that clear with its banning of men versus women games. Its leadership didn't believe women's football was a serious sport. The line of thinking was that what these women were doing was simply for entertainment and charitable purposes. It wasn't real athletics. Real football was a male space.

But then Dick, Kerr came along and helped make women's soccer an absolute sensation. The 53,000 audience attendance beat even that year's FA men's final. Instead of being excited about the possibility of the growth of the game it had helped establish, the leadership of the FA was piping mad, believing women were taking fans away from the men's game and—worse still—taking money away. The famous Boxing Day match proved one step too far.

The FA hadn't fully succeeded in making women's soccer go away last time, so now it decided to double down on its efforts. In December 1921, just a year after that match, the sixty male members of the FA got together and issued a terrible decree, directing clubs belonging to the association to refuse the use of their grounds for women's matches.

The FA based this decision on two preposterous beliefs:

1. Soccer was "unsuitable for females" based on recent biased medical studies which claimed that sports like soccer were dangerous for women's fertility.

2. The members were also suggesting that the players were pocketing more money than they should be to cover their expenses. Essentially, the FA was accusing the players of stealing money from charities! (They were not.)

The FA didn't ban women's soccer outright, but by banning any FA-associated team (which was pretty much all the men's teams) from letting ladies play at their venues, they stole the ground from under the women's feet. They had nowhere to play. Popular teams like Dick, Kerr were attracting tens of thousands to their matches, but people wouldn't continue to show up to random fields or pitches meant for different sports like rugby or cricket.

This was a disaster.

Dick, Kerr and all the other women who had relished in their time as female footballers were left stunned. By playing football in the factory leagues, they had felt free and powerful, they'd had real fun and created a one-of-a-kind sisterhood.

But now it was all being taken away from them. By the men from the FA. In a simple, solitary blow. It was that easy.

Although efforts were made to continue playing, the FA's decision was lethal. Within a few years, nearly all of the progress of the women's game was undone. For the third time in history, women's soccer had started and stopped. If the 1881 games lit a match for women's football, the British Ladies Football Club fanned the flames, and the Dick, Kerr era was a full-on blaze. But the FA had promptly snuffed it out.

Women's soccer was now banned.
And it would remain banned for fifty years.

Global Game: Australia

The incredible Dick, Kerr team inspired women worldwide, including in Australia. The first public women's match in Australia occurred in 1921, reportedly attracting a crowd of 10,000. Women wanted to have the same kind of fun those Dick, Kerr ladies in England were having, so they started their own clubs. They got around the little problem of not knowing how to play by attending introductory meetings where the game was explained to them with the help of illustrations on a blackboard. This led to the formation of the Matildas in 1978, Australia's elite national women's football team, which co-hosted the FIFA Women's World Cup in 2023.

5

Time Out:
A Fifty-Year Ban

Despite its meteoric rise for a short period of time, women's football in England was now outlawed. The FA had had enough of its growing popularity and decided to simply just do away with it. The female players who had grown to love the sport and relish being physically strong, who cherished their teammates, who had tasted the sweetness of victories and basked in the admiration of their many fans—did they just give up and hang up their cleats? Of course not! Yes, they lived in a world where men could easily take things away from women, but they weren't going to just walk away from this sport that meant so much to them.

Not without a fight.

The initial response to the FA's ban was anger, devastation, and disbelief. After all women had done to keep England going during the war—they had stepped up to work men's jobs, done their "second shifts" at home keeping house and supporting their families, raised thousands for charities—this is how they were thanked? And medical experts had felt women were strong enough to manage heavy machinery and hard labor jobs—but suddenly the war was over and women were back to being "the weaker sex"? It was time for defiance. And action.

Just three weeks after the FA's ban was issued, Dick, Kerr played a charity game against Fleetwood Ladies. Some adjustments had to be made—they played in a public park since all FA-associated venues were now closed to them, and they weren't reimbursed any expenses from money made at the ticket gate. The women played this match on their own dime so there couldn't be any more accusations of financial wrongdoing.

At this first game after the ban, thousands of loyal fans still showed up. To counteract the bogus doctors' opinions that the FA had relied on, the Dick, Kerr ladies invited dozens of new medical experts to witness a game with their own eyes. The team also invited members of the FA to the game—but none showed. All of the doctors who attended the match agreed that soccer was not actually damaging to women. One of them told the press that playing football wouldn't cause them any more harm than doing a lot of laundry.

The players couldn't stay silent either. In an interview, their captain promoted their plea:

> **Surely to goodness we have the right to play any game we think fit without interference from the Football Association!**
>
> –Alice Kell,
> Dick, Kerr defender, 1917–1928

They had the right to play any game they liked, especially the one they loved.

Beyond Dick, Kerr, female football players across England put their heads together on how to counteract the ban. Only five days after the FA's decree, twenty other English women's teams met in Liverpool and decided to form their own association with the hopes of keeping the sport alive. They called it the English Ladies Football Association. Surprisingly, it seems Dick, Kerr was not included—perhaps because the other teams were sour that it was likely their popularity that caused the ban for all of them. Or perhaps Dick, Kerr knew what it could accomplish on its own.

But none of the things these women did mattered in the end. The FA had wiped its hands clean of women's football. And that was that. Men still held the all the power when it came to this sport. The ban stood.

Despite the energy to keep women's soccer going in England, the effect of the ban was devastating. Female footballers no longer had proper grounds to play on—they had to settle for less-than-ideal pitches. None of the new venues could accommodate the thousands of fans who had attended Dick, Kerr's heyday matches. Things just weren't the same, and the crowds started to thin out. Without the acceptance, fun, and prominence they had before, many players left their teams, no longer interested in pursuing something so fraught. No new teams were being established, and fewer and fewer young girls saw themselves as future football stars. The outcome of this battle was heartbreakingly clear—the FA had won. The patriarchy was the victor. So many of the gains women had made in soccer were lost.

Thinking Outside the Box

The only team that stood a chance to survive the ban was, of course, Dick, Kerr. They were bona fide international celebrities. They continued to find ways to play, but also faced the same practical difficulties and dwindling interest. Some outside-the-box thinking was required. If they were unwelcome in England, perhaps they would be welcome abroad? A plan was hatched—Dick, Kerr would sail across the Atlantic and play women's teams in Canada and the United States.

So, in September 1922, Lily Parr, Alice Kell, Florrie Redford, and the other girls all boarded an ocean liner, giddy at this extraordinary opportunity for working women to explore the world and hopeful that there was still a future for women's football. But as soon as they arrived in Canada, they received crushing news. Inspired by England's FA, Canada's Dominion Football Association had passed its own resolution and denied permission for Dick, Kerr and any other women to play. "A woman was not built to stand the bruises gotten in football" one of the council members had argued.

SOCCER GAME

BETWEEN

Ladies' International Team

(Preston, England)

and selected team of

Washington Soccer Club

Scheduled for

AMERICAN LEAGUE PARK

TODAY, 3 P. M.

Will Start at 12:45 p.m.

So it will completed before

World Series Game

Pantomimed by

The Washington Times
THE NATIONAL DAILY

WHICH STARTS AT 2 P. M.

Those attending soccer game are invited to remain for World Series game as guests of The Times. See full page announcement elsewhere in this paper.

Disappointed but undeterred, the ladies of Dick, Kerr traveled south to the United States. There, they received more surprising news. There were no women's football teams in the U.S., as they had been led to believe. In fact, there weren't that many men's teams either. An entirely different sport was called football in this country—one with a very differently shaped ball—and, for men, it was a lot more popular than soccer.

For American women, the sport was nearly nonexistent. If Dick, Kerr wanted to play football in America, they would have to play men. Without any other choice, the players traveled up and down the East Coast of the United States playing men's clubs. They regularly attracted a good crowd and were victorious in a few games. Although the Dick, Kerr ladies got a trip of a lifetime, the tour was not what it promised, and it failed to inject any real hope for the future of women's soccer in England.

The Ban Spreads

What happened in Canada was one of the first signs of the contagiousness of the FA's actions. Other countries saw that the organization that had founded the sport was effectively prohibiting women from playing the game. Many other countries were unhappy about women taking over this sacred men's space, so when the FA called the sport dangerous and unsuitable for women, many similar associations jumped at the chance to proclaim it too. The ban served as an inspiration—the bad kind—to spread the stifling of women's soccer from England to the rest of the world.

Within a year, male-led football associations in Canada, Wales, Scotland, New Zealand, and Australia all put in place similar restrictions that excluded women, seriously impacting the growth of the sport. But it didn't stop there. Official bans were eventually issued in more countries, including West Germany, Spain, Brazil, and Nigeria. Each time, familiar reasons were given—soccer was simply "unladylike." The German Football Association went as far as saying: "In the fight for the ball, the feminine grace vanishes, body and soul will inevitably suffer harm." A banning fever had spread across the world—and it was a total disaster for women's football.

Brazil's Rebel *Futbolistas*

Nowhere in the world was women's soccer more prohibited than in Brazil. This may come as a surprise since the country has produced legendary players like Pelé, Ronaldo, Neymar, and Marta, who's considered the greatest women's player ever. But twenty years after England's ban, Brazil took things a step further. Instead of a football association, it was the nation's government that banned women from playing soccer—it was flat-out against the law.

In early twentieth-century Brazil, football was extremely popular and had always been well-loved by girls who played alongside their brothers, friends, and classmates in streets, fields, and patches of dirt. Organized women's soccer was pretty much nonexistent, but in the 1920s, some of the first female matches occurred—at the circus! Two teams of *futbolistas* playing against each other was considered prime entertainment. Just like in England, at first, women's soccer was treated as pure spectacle.

But by the 1930s, Brazilian women had organized and formed football clubs across the country. The state of the sport had all the marks of becoming a success: lots of players interested, the matches attracted fans and earned news coverage.

Like everywhere else in the world, women's football in Brazil had its critics. When it came to their reasoning, much of it was the same old story. "*Playing such a dangerous game could be damaging to women's fertility.*" And "*Women belonged at home.*" Brazilian critics also believed women playing soccer offended beauty standards. "*To be too muscular meant one was less beautiful*"—a major transgression in Brazilian culture. At a time when there was no acceptance of LGBTQ+ people, some accused women's football clubs of encouraging lesbian relationships between players. And because their uniforms involved the exposure of some skin (despite the fact most of the teams wore baggy, secondhand men's uniforms), the players were called lewd and were even accused of being prostitutes. The list isn't done yet—Brazilian critics also looked to the state of men's football at the time, which had a big problem with violence in the stands and on the pitch, and believed the women's game would inevitably be engulfed in the same anarchy. In other words, women had to pay for men's bad behavior. Having to put up with all of this was a lot for the players—and most certainly deterred many from picking up the sport.

But even with all the haters, by 1941, women's football in Brazil had become common, and even popular. But with success came more attention and more scrutiny. Just like with English soccer, this spelled bad news for female footballers. The Brazilian government had become more conservative and was primed to find ways to cling to traditional gender roles. When the National Sports Council approached it with a draft of a law that would formally ban women's soccer, just like many countries in Europe had, there was no hesitation. In August 1941, the Brazilian government passed Article 54, which made any girl who played soccer a lawbreaker. The official word was that the sport could "seriously damage the equilibrium" of women's "organ functions" and cause depression, which could lead to "rude and extravagant exhibitionism." Which was all another way of saying playing sports would ruin women's abilities to be mothers. And also cause their mental health to decline so much that they . . . would bother other people? The Brazilian government's ban applied not only to soccer, but to other sports labeled as violent like rugby, polo, and water polo. The ban didn't lay out any specific punishments, so it was largely left up to local governments to choose how to enforce it. This ban would remain in place for four decades.

Playing in the Shadows

Soccer was officially against the law. So what did Brazilian women do? Well, many just ignored it. They played on. It was impossible for Brazilians to escape the allure of football—it was just too popular and beloved in the culture. The government may have made it harder for women to play, but that just meant they had to get creative.

- Young girls found their own way to keep playing—some gathered at night, others dressed up in boys' clothing or played in discreet locations.

- Dilma Mendes, who went on to coach the Brazilian National Women's team during the 2023 World Cup, recounts that as a girl in the seventies, she would cut a deal with the boys she played with—if she bought them ice cream, then they had to tip her off if any police officers approached. And just in case, she would dig a ditch right next to the pitch so she could jump in it and hide at a moment's notice. Despite her best efforts, she still got hauled to the police station a few times where they'd question her and call her parents.

⬢ Legendary female football star **Sissi** didn't have access to real soccer balls as a young girl, so she improvised. She would decapitate her dolls and kick around their heads instead. Whatever worked!

For decades, young *futbolistas* played under the constant threat that their matches would be broken up, that they would be pulled away from the match by disapproving forces, be punished by their parents, or even be questioned at the police station.

During Brazil's ban, many women's football clubs were disbanded, but some rebel clubs remained active. Although official competitions were risky, the players relied on a tactic inspired by their English cohorts. Their matches were played as fundraisers for charity. This way, the organizers and teams could point to the good cause if the local government threatened to shut down the match. This was another example of how women could only participate in soccer if they didn't make money from it, unlike men who had the right to do so. Even though the clubs had community support, the police broke up some matches, anyway. Newspaper coverage was sparse and players' names were not mentioned—probably to help protect the identities of these women. Although no women were ever jailed in Brazil for playing football, plenty were detained and questioned. Brazilian female footballers clearly had the passion and the skills, but without the ability to legally play, the sport's growth was almost completely stunted.

In the decades following the ban, Brazil's *futbolistas* witnessed their men's national team become one of the best in the world, producing some of the greatest players in the world. Had they been allowed to play, could the women have become the best in their sport too? We'll never know, because while the men became legends, women were still playing in the shadows.

Even when Brazil received invitations to play abroad and in international tournaments, giving them an opportunity to form their own national team,

Brazil's Sissi survived the ban and went on the become a pioneer of women's football in Brazil. She wowed at the 1999 FIFA Women's World Cup, tying for top goal scorer. Here she is celebrating clinching a win in the quarter final match after scoring a Golden Goal in the 104th minute.

the women were forced to decline. There was so much promising female football talent in Brazil, but without the proper support and development, it all went wasted. Even though the law was finally changed in 1983, disapproval of women's football had become baked into Brazil's culture. It would take many years to undo the damage of the law and many years before Brazil caught up to other nations' programs, despite it being a country so well known for its love of football.

What Could Have Been

For the five decades that the ban lasted in many countries, the women's game stagnated. It's hard not to think about the stars, the incredible goals, and the amazing matches that could have been possible in this era. It's also hard not to think about all of those women and girls who, despite everything society was telling them, dreamed of playing football—and never really got a chance to.

While there is no doubt this is a sad era in women's soccer, there is another way to look at it. Despite sexist bans put in place by men and their institutions, women and girls around the world kept the sport alive. For decades, they continued to fall in love with the beautiful game. They continued to play, whether it was underground or in open defiance. They continued to push for a path forward. These women and girls from a multitude of countries kept the embers from the glorious Dick, Kerr era glowing, so that one day, women's soccer would blaze again.

Global Game: Japan

Women's soccer wasn't stagnant in all countries during the period of the ban. In Japan, the sport began to flourish during this time. Photos from 1916–1920 show schoolgirls playing soccer wearing *hakama*, a wide-pleated skirt tied at the high waist over their kimonos. After the 1964 Tokyo Olympics, interest in sports spiked, and the first women's clubs were formed in 1966. The national team, called *Nadeshiko* after a pink mountain wildflower, became World Cup champions in 2011.

58

Global Game: Afghanistan

In 2021, Afghanistan was seized by the Taliban, an extremist terrorist group that deprived women and girls of their rights in the name of Islamic fundamentalism. This included banning women from playing soccer and any other sport. Fearing for their safety, members of the national women's soccer team deleted their social media accounts, burned their kits, frantically attempted to erase their public identities, and desperately sought a way to safety. With the help of six nations, members of the national team and the women's soccer committee were evacuated to Australia, their new home. Although they were physically safe in Australia, the women's team was no longer recognized by the Afghanistan Football Federation, and as a result, were unable to play in any FIFA-sponsored matches, including the World Cup. The displaced Afghan players continue to train and put pressure on FIFA to allow them to play the game for which they have risked their lives.

The Afghan women's team celebrating a tournament win in 2013, before the Taliban retook control of Afghanistan and eliminated nearly all of women's freedoms.

6

Back in the Game

While women worldwide faced many hurdles for many years, men's soccer was given an easy road to flourish, becoming the most popular sport in the world.

In those years of the bans, many more countries founded their own men's football associations and the world's governing body for soccer, the *Federation Internationale de Football Association*, better known as FIFA, grew strong and important. Brilliant players emerged along with training programs filled with young boys aiming to become football stars. Pro leagues cropped up and communities developed passionate fandoms for their local clubs.

Men's soccer had become so huge that it was impossible to keep the sport totally hidden from women and girls—although we can be sure many would've preferred that. By the 1970s, there was potential for women's soccer to come back from the dead, the sport just needed a big boost to resuscitate it. Two major events happened that seemed to promise hope for a permanent future for the women's game. But was it enough to lock that future in?

Making up for Lost Time

In 1971, England's Football Association finally formally lifted its ban. Fifty years after it had first issued its decree, the association welcomed women back on its pitches, venues, and in its clubs. Many associations around the globe also lifted their prohibitions. So why had everyone changed their minds?

Well, the world had evolved in fifty years. Women had made many gains in achieving more equal rights in society. Since the 1921 FA ban, women across the world had earned the right to vote, own property, manage their own money, choose whom to marry, had more opportunities at work, and were no longer confined to overly restrictive clothing. By the 1970s, people had simply started to care less about whether or not women played soccer. It was no longer such a source of shock and outrage. Lots of women had just played anyway and, over the years, the enforcement of the bans got more and more lax. If no one cared enough to enforce the rules, what was the point of them?

The bans succeeded in seriously stunting the growth of the women's game and forcing it underground, but they had ultimately failed to fully keep women and girls from falling in love with the sport and finding ways to play. Women's soccer was officially back—but now the challenge was to make up for lost time. To be able to do that, the sport desperately needed to attract more players, to develop awesome talent, to create real clubs and leagues, and to get lots of funding to support all these efforts. The dream was that FIFA and the national federations would take control of the women's game to help all of this happen. The elimination of bans was definitely a step forward for women's soccer worldwide, but there was still a long journey ahead.

A World Cup . . . Unofficially

Despite the fact that women's soccer had scraped by during the ban years, and it was clear there was growing interest in the sport, FIFA still wanted to have nothing to do with it. To FIFA, soccer was still a sport for men and it preferred to ignore the fact that the women's game was developing on its own, with or without the organization's support. What would it take to show FIFA that women's soccer was worth paying attention to, to support with money and infrastructure, to help it flourish? What would make women's soccer impossible to ignore? The answer was: an unexpectedly huge success produced by intense rivals.

In 1970, FIFA didn't see the opportunity bubbling in women's soccer—but some Italian businessmen did. They also saw dollar signs where no one else did. A few years earlier, the Federation of Independent European Female Football (FIEFF), was formed by corporate backers of women's football clubs in Europe. Not one of the backers had anything to do with soccer before this venture. With money on their minds, FIEFF organized the first unofficial women's world cup in Italy that year, sponsored by a major Italian beverage company, Martini & Rossi. Seven teams participated—Italy, England, Switzerland, West Germany, Denmark, Austria and Mexico. Denmark ended up the winner of the Martini & Rossi Cup, making it the first-ever world champion in women's soccer. A whopping 40,000 people had shown up to the final match. Considering that the tournament had been cobbled together by people who didn't really know what they were doing, it was a success. Now the question was: could FIEFF pull off a second year of a world tournament and turn it into a really significant, money-making event?

FIEFF looked to Mexico, which had hosted a hugely popular FIFA Men's World Cup the year before as well as the Olympics in 1968. The country had stadiums that could accommodate large crowds and you could count on Mexican fans to show up in droves with enthusiasm. On top of that, a strong culture of female football clubs had developed in recent years. Mexico seemed like the perfect host for its unofficial world cup. The plan was set—the tournament would be held in Mexico over three weeks in August and September of 1971.

FIFA *hated* this idea. The world's governing body of soccer had two competing feelings—(a) it did not want to be involved in the women's game, but (b) if soccer was happening on a world level, it should be the organization involved or it should not be happening at all. An agitated FIFA tried to kill the tournament by banning Mexico's Football Federation from participating in an unsanctioned world tournament. Fortunately for women, FIFA's efforts were thwarted because it turned out that the two stadiums to be used—*Estadio Azteca* and *Estadio Jalisco*—were not owned or controlled by the Mexican Football Federation, and were therefore free and clear from FIFA.

It was game on.

The tournament hosted teams from Mexico, Argentina, Denmark, France, England, and Italy. Many of the players were only teenagers. England's squad included thirteen- and fourteen-year-olds. Mexico's star, Alicia Vargas, was fifteen. Susanne Augustesen, who played on the Danish team, was also fifteen and recalled having to beg for her parents' permission to miss a month of school. In their hometowns, most of the girls had been criticized or ridiculed for taking soccer seriously and for being too good at a "boy's sport." Some were even beaten by their parents or pulled off soccer fields by their ear. They had mostly only ever played on grass fields in public parks with a few dozen spectators. And many of them were traveling far away from home for the first time ever. The prospect of playing in an international tournament halfway across the world, right where their male soccer heroes had played just the year before, was beyond exciting. And Martini & Rossi was also paying for everything—travel, lodging, food, transportation, their uniforms, and cleats. The girls from Argentina had never even had enough money to own cleats before. It all sounded like a dream!

Before the tournament began, FIEFF put tons of work into promoting it. It was billed as a major, world-class event. Perhaps the corporate organizers didn't know much about soccer, but they knew a lot about advertising and marketing. Unfortunately, the focus of the promo wasn't so much on the elite athletics but, rather, the tantalizing appeal of attractive women playing soccer. Organizers promised that the players would look beautiful thanks to beauty salons in their locker rooms and revealing uniforms. The official mascot for the tournament was *Xochitl*, named after the indigenous word for "flower" and an ancient Aztec warrior queen, but reimagined for this audience as a cute pig-tailed girl in short shorts. The news reported that the tournament was "a double attraction—football and legs."

**Members of England's football squad pose with local musicians in Mexico City.
Spot Xochitl, the tournament's official mascot, on a poster behind them.**

In reality, there ended up being no beauty salons, the players' jerseys were loose-fitting and their shorts were a normal length. FIEFF seemed to have overstated the tournament's focus on sex appeal to sell tickets. It did deliver on painting the goalposts with pink and white stripes and stadium staff sporting pink uniforms.

Although the focus on sexualizing the players was demeaning, one positive spin on the organizers' approach is that they did not shy away from femininity. Things like pink goalposts may have undermined the real athleticism going on, but they also challenged long-held opinions that women playing soccer was unfeminine.

As always, female footballers had to put up with a lot to gain any ground.

When the young players touched down in Mexico, they were in for a total shock. Back home, no one cared that they were going to play in a soccer tournament, but thanks to an elaborate promotional campaign and widespread media coverage, these girls arrived in Mexico as stars. Imagine taking your first-ever plane ride and, on landing, you go from misunderstood outcast to celebrated hero. It was all so unexpected—and exciting.

The public just embraced us. We were always doing autographs. It was surreal.

–Leah Caleb,
England winger, 1971

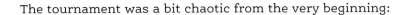

The tournament was a bit chaotic from the very beginning:

- Even for the qualifying matches, FIEFF seemed to be making it up as they went along. Some teams didn't even know they were playing qualifying matches—they only found out later that their win meant they were headed to Mexico to play in a world cup.

- The players dealt with harrowingly turbulent flights and dicey road trips.

- At one point during the tournament, the Danish squad's bus broke down and the team baked in the desert sun until the bus carrying the rival Italian team scooped them up.

- On a different occasion, the Argentinian team's bus collided with a van, injuring three players, including their top scorer, Elba Selva. That same team had acquired a new coach in the middle of the tournament.

- Players also dealt with some fan shenanigans. On the night before the semifinal between Mexico and Italy, hordes of Mexican fans gathered outside the Italian team's hotel, making as much noise as possible all night long so that the players couldn't get any sleep.

- Most gravely, the organizers were accused of rigging matches so that the host, Mexico, would end up in the final. Perfectly good goals were disallowed by referees, leading to physical altercations on the field and shady results.

Despite all of the chaos, the Mexican fans couldn't get enough of the tournament. Men, women and children showed up in huge numbers, enjoying not just the competitive matchups but the party atmosphere created by the good spirits and lively halftime entertainment. The first match of the tournament featured Mexico versus Argentina and attracted a totally unprecedented 80,000 Mexican spectators! Every match after that attracted an impressive audience. People from all over the country also tuned in to watch the games live on television.

The consensus among fans and the media was that the ladies were playing real-deal football. There were some naysayers who still felt the sport was too physical, too rough or that the players seemed like "men disguised as women." There was a lot of focus on the players' physical appearance, but overall, most were impressed by the high level of play and athleticism.

> ## The public arrived expecting to laugh at us, but by the time they left they had a completely different opinion.
>
> —Silvia Zaragoza,
> Mexico right winger, 1971

The players also loved the tournament. Never in their wildest dreams did they think playing soccer would lead them to such an extraordinary, unforgettable experience.

> ## It was something magical. You feel like you have wings.
>
> —Nicole Mangas,
> France defender, 1971–1973

Between the matches, practices, interviews, and autograph signing, they were also taking in Mexican culture, eating new foods, visiting heritage sites like Aztec pyramids and the Floating Gardens of *Xochimilco*, going to parties in their honor at embassies, staying in hotels, and basking in the sun poolside with their teammates, relishing in their good fortune. They also bonded with players from the other teams over their mutual talent and passion. And even better than all of this was the exhilaration of competing in the sport they so loved at the highest level, in front of tens of thousands of roaring fans. There was just no other feeling like it.

The final was to be between Mexico, the host country, and Denmark, the reigning champions. This particular matchup made for the perfect story arc and great headlines—even though fair play was probably not what actually got them there. The tournament had been a huge success so far and the organizers expected the final game to be its cherry on top—but the game almost didn't happen.

The members of the Mexican team had witnessed the tens of thousands of ticket-buying fans, the sponsorships, the media attention. They knew the public adored them—their fans had even given their star player, Alicia Vargas, the nickname *"La Pelé"* after the beloved male legend. Yes, they were grateful for all the support, but someone was making a lot of money off of this—*off of them*—and it wasn't any of the female soccer players.

Hall of Fame:
Alicia *'La Pelé'* Vargas

Alicia Vargas learned to play soccer on the streets of Guadalajara, Mexico, with her brothers and other boys. Despite her mother's disapproval, she honed her skills and became Mexico's greatest female player by the age of fifteen. She was nicknamed 'La Pelé" after the iconic male player—a huge compliment. Unfortunately, women's soccer wasn't well-supported in Mexico, and her team never qualified for a FIFA World Cup. Alicia retired in 1991 and worked as a physical education teacher for thirty years. In 2019, she was inducted into the International Football Hall of Fame.

Their team had been training for two years and they'd never been paid a dime. Male World Cup players didn't play for free—why should they? *La Pelé* and the rest of the Mexican team came together and gave an ultimatum—they were to be paid, or they wouldn't play in the final. Unfortunately, this is when the media soured on them. The news reported the Mexican team's standoff with disdain. *Who did these girls think they were?* The Mexican players went from being seen as the belles of the ball to ungrateful shrews who didn't deserve to be invited to the party. Sensing the public's shift in mood and feeling nervous about FIEFF's threat to simply put together an alternative team, the Mexican players announced that they had backed down and would compete in the final as an expression of appreciation for their fans. But the damage was done. The Mexican public no longer viewed them with the same fondness—they were now tainted with the high crimes of being women who spoke up for themselves and who dared to believe they were undervalued and under-compensated. The end to this tale was unfortunate, but what the brave Mexican players had attempted was remarkable—and also a precursor for a more victorious fight that would be taken up by female footballers two generations later.

On September 5, 1971, *Estadio Azteca* was filled to the absolute brim, with people pouring into the aisles. An astounding 112,500 fans showed up to witness the final game, making it the highest-attended women's sporting event in history—a record still held today. "When we walked out, the shouting and drumming was so loud that we couldn't even hear each other when we tried to talk," remembered Birte Kjems, Denmark's goalie. Despite their distaste for the Mexican team's attempt to stand up for themselves, fans still wanted to see the grand finale of the tournament. In the end, Denmark was champion once again, beating the host nation 3-0 thanks to an epic hat trick by the teenage Susanne Augustesen. Even though the Danes had trounced the home team, the crowd regaled them with applause and the girls were handed a trophy featuring an angel standing on top of a soccer ball.

How did they celebrate? "We had a bath in pink champagne!" recalled Birte. "I don't know where it came from, I didn't even know pink champagne existed, but there was lots of it after the final!"

With the help of top goalscorer Lise Lene Nielson, Denmark secured its spot as champion of the 1971 Cup.

With the tournament now over, the players had to return to their countries. They hadn't made any money (except for a few enterprising women who had charged for their autographs), but they had had the experience of a lifetime. The girls rode high all the way back to their native lands but when they arrived, most faced a major comedown. Back home, no one really knew about their success or understood their surreal experience. People didn't believe the stories they told them. The English girls ended up being ashamed of even talking about it. On their return, England's FA had handed Leah Caleb and her teammates each a personal six-month ban for participating in an unsanctioned tournament. The young players felt like they had done something wrong. It must have been so hard to return to their normal lives, many as high school students, where their skills in soccer were underappreciated and even mocked. While they may never have felt the thrills of Mexico again, they did have the magical memories of those three weeks in history when they were international superstar athletes.

The Danish squad returned home from Mexico as world champions.

The 1971 cup had been a massive success. FIEFF had made lots of money. Female footballers had finally had the opportunity to showcase their impressive skills to the world. Once again, women's soccer, for a brief moment in time, was wildly popular. This time, captivating the nation of Mexico. Shouldn't this success have launched something big for women's soccer? Given it the boost it finally needed to become a permanent fixture in sports? Surprisingly, sadly, disappointingly—it wasn't. One major reason was that FIEFF had clearly rigged matches so that the tournament could maximize profits and keep the host country happy. As desperate as women's soccer was to develop, it had to do so legitimately. By prioritizing money over athletics, FIEFF had lost its credibility and its tenuous hold on the sport. This would be their last world cup, and it would be all but forgotten for decades.

And then there was FIFA. Its leaders had watched what was happening in Mexico from afar, irked. After the cup was over, the organization knew it could no longer turn its back on women's soccer. It also did not want an unsanctioned tournament to happen ever again. A lasting legacy of the 1971 unofficial world cup is that it finally got FIFA to pull women's soccer into its orbit. With FIFA officially involved, FIEFF was officially out. FIFA sent the message out worldwide that national federations should now "take control" of women's soccer. This sounded like it should be a good thing, right? Well, it was yet another mixed bag for female footballers. Having national federations officially supporting women's soccer was a big legitimizing step. But, at first, many countries' federations didn't actually put any money or efforts into developing the sport. Women's soccer couldn't grow without the water and sunshine that substantial funding provided.

Despite being a one-hit wonder, the 1971 cup did have a legacy—it demonstrated the high level of play female footballers were capable of, helped to inspire future international tournaments, and it finally convinced FIFA to care about women's soccer. The tournament had also proved that women's soccer could be commercially successful—but this was a truth that would also be forgotten for several decades.

Dick, Kerr's heyday and the 1971 cup were both high-profile, flashy moments in women's soccer, but neither had succeeded in solidifying a future. What the sport really needed was something major to happen on a fundamental level. Deep-in-the-ground success was harder to erase than single triumphant moments. Without that strong foundation, women's soccer couldn't really grow.

While female footballers were showing what they were made of in Mexico, just north of the border, something major was brewing.

Title IX
and Awakening
a Sleeping Giant

Before 1972, if you were an American high school girl who wanted to play sports, your options were limited. High schools across the U.S. had plenty of competitive sports teams for their male students, but not so many for the girls. You were lucky if your school offered one of the sports that were popular for girls at the time—field hockey, softball, volleyball, or basketball. If you wanted to play soccer (or even knew what it was), forget about it—there were no girls' soccer teams. Your school might not offer any teams for girls at all, so your only option would be to scrape together the courage to try out for the boys' team. And that's only if they'd let you—many schools did not allow girls to play on boys' teams. Sports were still seen as a masculine activity, and the development of girls' sports was very low on the priority list. If a school did have sports teams for girls, they often didn't have uniforms or had to use hand-me-downs from the boys' teams. A girls' team often only had a coach if someone volunteered for the role for free. The teams had to make do with where to play and where to change their clothes. In comparison, the boys' teams had uniforms, plenty of equipment, paid coaches, use of gyms, weight rooms, sports fields, and locker rooms. As for sports scholarships— they were definitively not for girls, closing the door on that particular path to a good education.

This discrimination against female students didn't just apply to sports—it extended to all areas of public education in the United States. Certain classes, special programs, scholarships, and opportunities were all closed to girls. Universities and graduate schools didn't want lots of women making up their student population and made it nearly impossible for female students to be admitted. It seemed the whole American educational system prioritized male students. Why? It went back to the age-old myth that women were the weaker sex and better suited for a life at home. The theory at the time was that boys were one day going to be the breadwinners for their households, so of course, the opportunities should be better. To put it plainly, boys and young men were given more chances to succeed. But how could girls and young women ever change this unjust system if they were never given the opportunity to pursue their interests or to develop and showcase their talents?

The female students of America needed a strong, earth-shattering law to dismantle this rigged system and protect them from discrimination.

They deserved equal opportunities.

Breaking barriers

To make that happen, they needed representatives in the federal government to champion their interests. In 1971, they got their champions—Congresswomen Edith Green of Oregon and Patsy Takemoto Mink of Hawaii. They also had the critical support of a male senator from Indiana, Birch Bayh. Both Congresswomen Green and Mink were deeply familiar with discrimination in education, as they both had faced—and broke—barriers along their paths. But they knew they were the exceptions. Things had to change, and they were in the position to make that happen.

> **"What you endure is who you are. I can't change the past. But I can certainly help somebody else in the future, so they don't have to go through what I did.**
>
> —Patsy Takemoto Mink,
> Congresswoman, Hawaii

Congresswomen Edith Green (left), and Patsy Takemoto Mink (right).

Together, the congresswomen helped draft a law that became known as Title IX. The idea was simple—require all schools receiving government funds (which included all public schools and universities) to give equal opportunities to female and male students. Title IX was part of a larger education bill and its portion contained only thirty-seven words. Thirty-seven monumental, consequential words:

"No person in the United States, shall, on the basis of sex, be excluded from participation in, be denied the benefits of, or be subject to discrimination under any educational program or activity receiving Federal financial assistance."

Although the bill received some pushback in Congress, with the congresswomen and Senator Bayh pushing for it, it was ultimately passed and signed into law in 1972 by President Richard Nixon. This was a huge victory for American women. Title IX would ultimately become one of the most consequential and effective laws that protect women from gender discrimination in America.

At the time Title IX was passed, it wasn't really viewed as a law that would have a great impact on sports. It was celebrated more for how it affected educational opportunities and school admissions. The law didn't even mention sports. But after Title IX came into effect, and the federal government, schools, and universities had to figure out how to comply with it, it became clear that the law had a big impact on school sports and sports scholarships. If schools were going to receive the federal funding that was critical to their continued existence, they had to make major changes to their athletics programs.

Schools and universities across the United States were panicking—to be in compliance with Title IX they had to fairly distribute funding to both boys' and girls' sports. There was a lot of confusion at first. Did that mean boys and girls had to play on the same teams? Play on the same fields? Did the schools have to buy them the same equipment? Would they have to cut boys' teams to make room for girls' teams? Ultimately, the schools realized they had to create more opportunities and provide equitable funding of girls' athletics. That meant establishing more girls' sports teams. Given many schools had none to start with, this was a big shift.

When it came to adding new girls' teams, schools were looking for inexpensive options that wouldn't take too much money away from the boys' teams that already existed. That's when soccer—a sport most Americans didn't really know much about—started to look very shiny and attractive. Think about it: soccer is not an expensive game to play. All schools needed to get going were some balls, a field, and two goals. The rules of the game weren't very complicated. It was easy to learn and so could draw a lot of new players. The sport also fielded a large roster of twenty-plus girls, making it easier for schools to fulfill their Title IX requirements. To Americans, soccer had another thing going for it—it felt more feminine than some of the country's beloved, more violent sports, like tackle football. This was funny, given that in most other countries, soccer was the most popular contact sport and considered deeply masculine. But in the United States, compared to the tackles and hard knocks of its football, soccer seemed gentler, and therefore suitable for girls and women. The boys of America were preoccupied with other sports, which freed up soccer as one where girls could get in on the game without sexist blockades.

Making it Mainstream

In those first years after Title IX became law, the changes were slow-going. It took a while for schools to get their acts together, create new teams for girls, and figure out how to fund them. But the interest was there—girls and young women came out in droves to take advantage of all the new athletic opportunities that they now had. The hidden world of school sports was open to them—they were learning what it felt like to compete athletically, to feel physically strong, to be members of a team, and to form special bonds with your fellow teammates. It was electrifying for many American girls and young women. Things weren't perfect yet—boys' teams still had better uniforms, better equipment, better fields and locker rooms, but real progress was being made. And now armed with Title IX, female students who wanted to create opportunities for themselves had an ultra-powerful tool to put pressure on their schools that were falling short of the law's requirements.

For the first time in American history, many middle and high school girls were strapping on shin guards, tying up cleats, and learning the rules of soccer. Previously, soccer had only really been played in immigrant communities that had imported the beloved sport of their homelands—but now, thanks to Title IX, it was on its way to becoming mainstream.

At the university level, soccer went from a niche sport that was solely played at women's colleges to one that was more widespread. Early university teams like the University of North Carolina-Chapel Hill barely had any other teams to play against in their first years, so they had to resort to playing local high school teams. It took a few years for women's soccer to catch fire at the college level, but when it did, universities had no shortage of other schools to compete against. And that meant more college soccer scholarships were available for women, creating a fresh pathway for female students to get higher education.

It wasn't just older girls and young women taking up the sport—little kids started playing too. American parents realized that all they had to do was buy some cleats and shin guards and their kids were ready to play. Parents also loved that it was a team sport and that there was a low chance of injury, especially compared to other popular sports. Another great thing was that the sport didn't favor physical bulk like football or height like basketball—soccer was for every kid.

Title IX had awakened a sleeping giant. America was more than one hundred years late to the soccer party—but now that middle schools, high schools, colleges and universities, and even suburban parents had embraced the game, the U.S. had become the life of the party—at least when it came to women's soccer. From 1972 on, there was a domino effect in the U.S.: young girls played in rec leagues or club teams, which led many to play on their high school teams, which led some to play

Hall of Fame:
Patsy Takemoto Mink

Patsy Takemoto Mink was the first Asian American woman elected to the U.S. Congress. As a high school student on the island of Maui, Hawaii in the 1940s, she was valedictorian and class president. Patsy initially aspired to become a doctor, but she faced rejection from medical schools which had few openings for women at the time. Undeterred, she decided to go to law school and become a lawyer. After being elected to Congress in 1965, she fought for gender and racial equality. Patsy was known for urging her colleagues in Congress to understand and address the deep-seated injustices of sexism. One day, she and two other female congresswomen protested by demanding access to the men's-only House of Representatives gym, seeking equal treatment. After Patsy died in 2002, Title IX was renamed the Patsy T. Mink Equal Opportunity in Education Act.

on college and university teams, which led the best players to become national team players and pursue ways to play as adults. With such growing interest and lots of new players, more opportunities were created for girls and women to play and more programs were instituted to develop talent. The players were getting better and better. The U.S. universities had an elaborate and elite collegiate sports system unlike any other country, and within a short time, women's soccer teams went from existing at a handful of schools to hundreds. To those beyond its borders, the U.S. offered a chance for women to play soccer and get a good education—something that other countries couldn't offer. By the 1980s, the United States was offering the best environment for women's soccer in the world—and it was only getting better. Title IX had gotten the ball rolling on all of this. It did not have an immediate impact on women's soccer but it had a lasting impact. It helped raise the profile of soccer in the United States and ultimately led to the establishment of the team that would one day become synonymous with the sport of women's soccer.

8

The First FIFA
Women's
World Cup

In earlier eras, the question was whether women should play soccer at all. For decades, many people's answer was no. But attitudes changed, and women were eventually allowed to play. And then a new question emerged—just as discriminatory: are women *good enough* to play? For twenty years after 1972's unofficial first Women's World Cup, female footballers were asked to prove themselves over and over and over again. They had to show that they deserved the world's attention, investment, and development. That they were too good to ignore. That they should have their own FIFA World Cup, just like the men.

While men's soccer had been handed a world cup by FIFA without question, women's soccer was forced to fight for the privilege. For those twenty years, trailblazing players worked hard to prove that they were fierce competitors and world-class athletes.

The first trial was in 1975, when Hong Kong hosted the first Asian Women's World Cup featuring Singapore, Thailand, Hong Kong, Malaysia, Australia, and New Zealand. Thousands of spectators showed up, and the ladies showed off their sharp skills in thrilling games. As a result, women's soccer earned itself a new international opportunity—an invitation-only mini world cup called a "*mundialito*," hosted by Japan in 1981. It went so well that four more *mundialitos* were organized—

all hosted by Italy between 1984 and 1988. Teams from Italy, Japan, Denmark, England, Belgium, West Germany, China, Brazil, and the United States all participated. The players loved these opportunities to form national teams for the first time and play against other nations' best footballers. FIFA watched from afar—still skeptical—but slowly becoming more and more convinced of the relevance of women's soccer. The players' greatest wish was that the success of these tournaments would be enough to convince FIFA to let them have a world cup of their own. A FIFA World Cup would be the ultimate recognition for their sport.

A Courageous Plea

In 1984, FIFA got a direct plea from Ellen Wille, the sole female delegate from Norway's Football Association. She was attending FIFA's national congress in Mexico City, where members of national federations gathered to review football's annual state of affairs. Ellen was livid. Women's football was barely mentioned a single time in FIFA's annual report. When it was time to take comments, Ellen stepped up to the podium as the only woman in the cigar-smoke-filled room of 145 delegates and all of FIFA's top brass—it was the first time a woman had ever done so. Unafraid, she wasted zero time in pointing out the report's snub, and that wasn't all. "I also said it was high time the women had their own World Cup and took part in the Olympic Football Tournament," Ellen recalled. While a lot of members of FIFA and the different federations were annoyed by Ellen's comments, one key person agreed—FIFA President João Havelange. This surprised many, but even more were surprised when his number two, Sepp Blatter, replied "Madame, I will accept the challenge. You will see. We will go for the organization of a Women's World Cup."

Ellen Wille's courageous plea, plus the players' love of the game, their talent, and their persistence shifted opinions. But was all of that enough for FIFA at the time? Not quite. Before FIFA would agree to host an official world cup, it required female footballers to prove themselves yet again. In 1988, FIFA organized a trial international tournament in Guangzhou, China, giving it the name: the FIFA International Women's Football Tournament. If the tournament was successful, the organization would put on a real-deal World Cup. Twelve teams showed up eager and ready to wow, knowing so much more than a trophy was at stake.

The teams covered six continents, demonstrating what a global sport women's soccer had become. Over the course of the twelve-day tournament, 250,000 people showed up to watch the women. Ellen Wille's mighty Norwegian team was crowned the champion. Finally, FIFA was sufficiently impressed.

The time had come for women's soccer. Just two weeks after the tournament in Guangzhou, FIFA greenlit a women's world cup for 1991. But, as usual, there was a catch. The organization was afraid of bestowing its sacred "World Cup" name upon this brand-new women's event, so it opted for a different name. A mouthful of a name. The tournament was officially called: the 1st FIFA World Championship for Women's Football for the M&M's Cup.

M&M's? Like the candy? The tournament's only sponsor was Mars, the company that manufactured M&M's. The name maybe didn't have the grandeur or the esteem of a "FIFA World Cup," but the event was a global tournament put on by FIFA, featuring the best of the best in women's soccer from around the world. The ladies would take it!

This was the opportunity that they, and so many generations before them, had worked so hard for.

The title of the tournament wasn't the only thing the players had to settle for. FIFA decided to shorten the length of a regulation match from ninety minutes to eighty minutes. "They were afraid our ovaries were going to fall out if we played ninety!" U.S. captain April Heinrichs joked (but was kind of serious). To add insult to injury, FIFA even discussed using a smaller size 4 ball instead of the traditional size 5, despite the fact the players had only ever used a size 5. Thankfully, FIFA decided against this particular modification. It did issue a list of rules related to the players' appearances. "[A]n enormous amount of attention [was] paid to how much jewelry we were wearing," recalled April. "You couldn't wear a ring, couldn't have anything at all, which was fine . . . even though at the time the men were wearing more jewelry than we were." Despite all of FIFA's questionable judgments that seemed anywhere from borderline to overtly sexist, for the players, playing in this first world cup was still an absolute dream come true.

Future Legends

The host of the tournament was again Guangzhou, China. Twelve teams qualified for the first women's world cup: China, Japan, Chinese Taipei, Brazil, New Zealand, Nigeria, Denmark, Germany, Italy, Norway, Sweden, and the United States. Twenty-six matches across five cities in southern China took place over two weeks in November 1991.

Women's soccer was still a relatively new sport in all of the competing countries, with plenty of skeptics around still posing hurdles. Thanks to Title IX, the United States had gained the most ground in the past twenty years, establishing an elaborate college program that even attracted players from other countries. The 1991 U.S. women's national team represented the first generation of women who had grown up benefitting from this law, and the players were sometimes referred to as "the Title IX babies." You'd think that the country that had one of the best women's soccer programs in the world would have fancy uniforms and a bevy of coaches. But heading into the world cup, the U.S. national team had no full-time coaching staff. Even their head coach, Anson Dorrance, was borrowed from the University of North Carolina-Chapel Hill. And the players' uniforms? Castoffs from the men's team. Which was better than their usual hand-me-downs from a U.S. boys youth squad. They had to buy their own cleats.

The United States squad arrived in Guangzhou as one of the favorites to win. Their journey had been extra long, as FIFA opted to save money by having their plane make several stops in Europe along the way to pick up other teams. One of the American stars was Michelle Akers, a forward who stood a towering 5'10" and whose face was framed by a curly mane of hair, evoking the fierce lioness that she was. Her teammates lovingly called her "Mufasa" after the *Lion King* character. She was joined up front by captain April Heinrichs and Carin Jennings. Also on the team were a nineteen-year-old Mia Hamm and twenty-four-year-old Brandi Chastain, who were early in their journeys to becoming future legends.

The players from all of the teams were surprised to be greeted by lots of media and cameras at the Guangzhou airport. Back in their home countries, women's sports

Brandi Chastain fights for a through ball during U.S.A.'s group stage victory over Japan in the 1991 Women's World Cup.

didn't normally get that kind of press. They were even more surprised when the streets from the airport to their hotels were lined with banners, big floral statues of women playing soccer, and people cheering them on. The people didn't even seem to know which team any of them were on, but it didn't matter—there was real, palpable excitement for the tournament. And the players were beyond surprised when up to three thousand people would show up to watch their training sessions. Wanting to get their autographs and photos and touch them and hug them.

Was this tournament going to be a big deal?

> **From the very first day we could feel 'Man, this is something quite different' to what we'd ever seen before. There were more journalists when we trained than we had for actual games here in Europe.**

–Keld Gantzhorn,
Denmark head coach, 1988–1996

Playing Their Hearts Out

Despite some of the signs that FIFA was treating this tournament as a second-class World Cup, the opening ceremony did not disappoint. One thousand ornately-costumed performers took to the field, executing an intricate dance complete with thousands of lights, floating lanterns, and in the center of it all, a giant mechanical phoenix. A fitting symbol for a sport that had risen from the ashes of a fifty-year ban. After the ceremony, it was time for China and Norway to kick off the competition. Every player was crackling with nerves. Some had only ever played in front of hundreds, nowhere near the 65,000 in attendance that day.

The stakes felt so high.

One of China's players was forward Sun Wen, who was eighteen at the time. "Before our first match, I was so nervous that I didn't know what to do," she remembered. "All I could think was . . . breathe." Despite the stress, the Chinese team did not disappoint their many fans in the stands and trounced Norway 4-0. Chinese defender Ma Li had the honor of scoring the very first goal in women's World Cup history in the twenty-second minute of the game.

From there, the tournament went into full swing. Games were sold out and people who couldn't make it in lingered outside, creating an electric atmosphere for the players. Even though the women had been deemed as lacking the stamina to last the full ninety minutes that men played, they were scheduled to compete in matches at a breakneck pace. Teams had only one day to recover from the exhausting athletic feat of playing their hearts out in world cup matches. During the men's World Cup, the players often had four days to recover between games.

"It was harder than any tournament a man would ever play," Michelle Akers declared.

And there were many more differences between how male and female World Cup players were treated.

Nigeria goalkeeper Oyeka Anna Agumanu and Omon-Love Branch (No. 5)
try to stop German Heidi Mohr's attack.

- The women's teams bunked multiple players together in rooms at hotels while men were lodged in their own rooms at nicer hotels.

- The U.S. players were only given $10 a day to spend on food. Many players on the U.S. team were too nervous to shock their stomachs with local delicacies, so for the two weeks they were in China, they ate mostly pasta and peanut butter on bread, which they packed from home. They also ate lots of free Snickers bars—one nice perk of the Mars sponsorship.

- None of the teams were paid any money to play, there was no prize money for the victors, and there were no sponsorship deals.

This financial bit was the biggest difference between male and female players.

Men were compensated for their athleticism while women were expected to play only for the love of the game.

Most of the women balanced being on their national teams with full-time jobs or school.

All of the players noticed the differences between the men's World Cup and their own. It bothered them but, at the time, they didn't have much leverage to change any of it. Women's sports had always been secondary to men's—this was nothing new. They were being afforded this incredible opportunity to play the sport they loved and trained so hard for. They didn't know if they were going to get to play in another tournament like this ever again. The female athletes were determined to show the world just what they were capable of and believed that they could push the sport forward by playing their best. Right now, their focus was on winning.

Hall of Fame:
Hege Riise

Hege Riise is considered Norway's best female football player ever and one of the greatest to come out of Europe. Despite not being a striker, Hege was a prolific goalscorer. Her incredible skills as a midfielder helped her national team win football's three biggest tournaments: the Euro Cup, the Women's World Cup, and the Olympics—a super rare achievement held by only a handful of footballers of any gender. On top of that, she led her WUSA team, the Carolina Courage, to clinch the league title in 2002. One of the early pioneers in women's soccer, she was also one of the first Norwegian women to play for a Japanese club, during a time where very few Europeans sought to play in Asia. As usual, Hege's presence meant victory, and she helped secure the league title and cup for Nikkon Securities Dream Ladies FC. After Hege retired in 2006, she went on to coach the very team she led to historic victories. She remains a beloved and respected presence in women's football today.

After twenty-five hard-fought matches, the championship game was between the United States and Norway—the up-and-coming powerhouse versus the 1988 trial tournament champ. The countries already had a heated rivalry. Their squads had come head-to-head several times in previous years. In front of 63,000 fans, these two teams competed in the most important match yet in all of women's soccer. It was by far the biggest crowd any of the players had ever played in front of. They felt anxious, proud, and ravenous for the championship title. Laser-focused on the job they had to do, the players did not even have the bandwidth to fangirl when the iconic Pelé shook each player's hand before kickoff.

Despite an embarrassing loss to to China in the opening game, the Norwegian team, featuring midfielder Hege Riise—who would become Norway's best female football player ever—had fought its way to the final.

The U.S. team had won all of its games—its three-pronged offense of Michelle Akers, April Heinrichs, and Carin Jennings was dubbed the "triple-edged sword" by the Chinese press. The U.S. scored first after a sweet header by Akers, but her goal was matched eight minutes later by Norway's Linda Medalen. At halftime, the rivals were tied. In the U.S. locker room, a lot of shouting was going on—everyone was wrecked with nerves and adrenaline. On her way back on to the field, Michelle Akers was approached by one of the coaches, Tony DiCicco. "Mich, you're gonna have to win the game," he told her simply, yet firmly. Michelle remembers thinking, "It wasn't 'C'mon, you can do it.' It was one of those truths. Inside, it struck me. Like 'Yes, I am gonna have to win this. I know.'"

With two minutes left to go in the game, Michelle did something every soccer player dreams of—she scored the winning goal in a FIFA World Cup Championship Final.

> **It's the goal you think of as a kid. Last two seconds of the game. Open goal. Defenders are rushing down. The whole world is watching. 'Can you score?' It was like that. And I did it.**
>
> —Michelle Akers,
> U.S. midfielder, 1985–2000

Michelle Akers, Carin Jennings, and Julie Foudy celebrate winning the very first FIFA Women's World Cup.

The United States was officially the first Women's World Cup champion. When the final whistle blew, they threw their arms in the air, jumped, and hugged each other. It was the biggest moment of their lives. Captain April Heinrichs was handed the very first Women's World Cup trophy, and she hoisted it above her head victoriously. The U.S. national team was on top of the world. They had won the championship and two individual players were recognized for their incredible skills. Michelle Akers had scored an amazing ten goals during the tournament, which earned her the Golden Boot award, and Carin Jennings received the Golden Ball for being MVP of the entire tournament. On the bus ride back to the hotel, they danced and sang Queen's "We Are the Champions" at the top of their lungs. Back at their hotel, in a gesture of good sportsmanship, the Swedish team had arranged their medals to spell "U.S.A." The American women celebrated their victory late into the night.

Life as Usual . . . For Now

The U.S. team left Guangzhou as world champions, but when they arrived back in the United States, there were no fans waiting for them, just two members of the press. They had left the fanfare and media frenzy behind in Guangzhou. "Nobody knew what was going on," Michelle explained. "It was interesting . . . we just did this huge thing, and you come home and it's life as usual." Chinese media had broadcast all of the matches, but they were only available in the U.S. on a cable channel that not that many people had. Needless to say, a ticker tape parade for this team was not in the works. The players had thought their win would be a game-changer—that people would start caring and paying attention to and funding women's soccer. But that clearly was not the case. After the biggest moment of their lives, the players returned to their universities to take their final exams or went back to their full-time jobs. The $500 bonus the U.S. Soccer Federation awarded them didn't go very far. Although they were playing at a professional level, without being paid to play, they were considered only amateurs.

The players did receive one special honor—they were invited to the White House where they got to shake hands with President George H.W. Bush, who had played soccer in high school and college. He even headed a ball back and forth with April Heinrichs for the occasion. At the ceremony, the team didn't hesitate to state their next goal with the President and the press— to get women's soccer in the Olympics.

Hall of Fame:
Michelle Akers

Michelle Akers played in U.S. women's national team's very first match in 1985. Standing at 5'10", she used her height to her advantage and was known for her physical and aggressive playing style. She was a respected leader on the teams she played on and admired for her incredible determination, even when faced with injuries and chronic fatigue syndrome. Although she started off as a striker, she later became a midfielder. Some of her goal-scoring records still stand today. She was a true pioneer in women's soccer, advocating for the sport's recognition and pushing for more equal treatment. In 2000, she was named FIFA's Female Player of the Century and was inducted into the U.S.'s National Soccer Hall of Fame in 2004.

When it came to the all-important FIFA, the organization was very pleased with how well the tournament had gone. So pleased, that it retroactively gave it the official moniker. So even though it technically wasn't a FIFA Women's World Cup when it was played, it is now formally remembered as the first one. Determined female footballers around the world had passed trial after trial, winning over everyone who was watching every single time. From now on, they would get to play a FIFA World Cup every four years, just like the men. Yes, it was true their World Cup wasn't funded like the men's cup, but this was a monumental win for the sport. And the cherry on top? The athletes were so impressive that just five years later, women's soccer was played during the Summer Olympics for the very first time in Atlanta, Georgia. This generation of "Title IX babies" and other female footballers around the world had succeeded in advancing their sport, but they still had so far to go. At the time, it didn't seem possible that women's soccer could ever be a big deal. But, in just a few years, everything would change.

American sports fans first showed real excitement for women's soccer during the 1996 Olympic Games in Atlanta, Georgia.

Fashion on the Field

Soccer attire has come a long way since the very first women stepped out on to the pitch in 1881. What women have worn to play hasn't been just a fashion statement or an athletic necessity. Over the years, women's kits have told the story of inequities, protests against discrimination, and the development of more power and respect.

1881　Knickerbockers and Heels

The first female footballers wore whatever they could to be ready to play. They donned blousy tops and either loose-fitting knee-length pants or skirts held up by belts. These pants, known as "knickerbockers" or "bloomers" were seen as controversial womenswear at the time, as they were associated with American feminists and women who needed something more practical to wear to—*gasp!*—partake in physical activities. Instead of shin guards and cleats, the players wore stockings and heeled boots. Today, this outfit seems far from pitch-perfect.

1890s　Ditching the Corset

In the days of the British Ladies Football Club, players still wore blouses and divided skirts which had two distinct wide legs as bottoms. Like male players, they now wore football boots, ankle pads, and shin guards. They pinned up their hair and wore caps, as covered heads were the look of the times. The most revolutionary—and feminist—change at the time was that players abandoned their tight-fitting corsets. Addressing those who were aghast, Lady Florence took to the press and defended their choice of uniform—declaring any other form of dress ridiculous. When it came to women playing sports, the suffocating grip of the corset just didn't make sense . . . or seem healthy.

Long Story Short

By the 1920s, gone were the bloomers and split skirts, the players now wore above-the-knee shorts. While the exposure of "so much" bare leg certainly upset some people, the players' legs were now freed up for more movement and agility. It may seem like a small change, but this adjustment in uniform helped women level up their game and skills, which definitely contributed to development of the adoring fandom of the era.

Dick, Kerr sporting their iconic black and white uniforms, including the shorts that allowed them to move as the real athletes they were.

1970s   (Not Quite) Made to Measure

In the seventies, there was no soccer gear specifically designed for women. What was available had been created with men in mind, without considering the differences in men's and women's bodies. Shin guards designed for men didn't fit most women, so many—even at the college level—opted not to wear them, increasing the likelihood of injury. Men's cleats gave women blisters, and the socks were so big, women pulled on regular old tube socks instead. It would take years before gear was designed to fit women's bodies properly. While women's soccer equipment has come a long way, there is still a need for more research into creating gear tailored to female athletes' bodies, just like men have.

1985   Making Do with Hand-Me-Downs

The very first U.S. women's national team wore hand-me-downs from the U.S. men's and youth teams. For their first appearance in an international tournament, a "*mundialito*" held in Italy, players and staff members stayed up late the night before their flight, making do with what they had by cutting up and sewing the uniforms so they would better fit a woman's body and help the athletes perform at their best.

1999 · A New Way to Show Support

It was the sports bra seen around the world. The image of Brandi Chastain celebrating her epic winning goal, her torn-off jersey in hand and fists in the air in triumph, is considered one of the most iconic images in all of sports history. This moment actually caused backlash, with some uncomfortable with Brandi's choice to disrobe, and others buying into the cynical theory that it was a planned act to get a Nike sponsorship deal. However, many people saw it as a genuine expression of victory. For many girls and women, it was empowering to see such strength expressed in a uniquely feminine way. Brandi always maintained it was an impromptu act of euphoria. She was emulating her male soccer heroes' celebrations. Today, she remains proud of this moment: "I hope that young girls who see that picture see a little bit of themselves. You know, they see the strength and power. A lifelong journey, the willingness and confidence it takes to be seen." In 2019, a bronze statue immortalizing the moment was placed outside the Rose Bowl Stadium in Pasadena, California. The most famous sports bra in the world currently hangs framed in Brandi's home office.

Early 2000s–Present · Hair Wear

The beloved headband worn by female footballers—professional, youth, and everyone in between—isn't actually a headband at all, it's a medical gauze called pre-wrap. Originally designed to protect skin from irritating athletic tape, pre-wrap's softness, stretchiness, and slightly tacky texture make it perfect for keeping an athlete's hair in place during training or a match. Many players have adopted pre-wrap as a hair accessory, either rolled up or laid flat, and in a variety of colors. The most famous pre-wrap wearer is the United States' Alex Morgan, who started wearing it in pink as a youth player so her parents could easily spot her on the field. Alex even had a sponsorship deal with the pre-wrap company, Mueller Sports Medicine.

Uniforms have become a way for players to make a statement of protest against injustice. In 2020, the U.S. women's national team wore their warm-up kits inside out to call out their federation amid a pay equality lawsuit. In 2023, the Canadian women's soccer team was in its own pay equity battle with its federation. The players were on strike, but Canada Soccer gave them an ultimatum: play in the SheBelieves Cup or face legal consequences. The players took to the pitch wearing purple warm-up shirts emblazoned with "ENOUGH IS ENOUGH," sending a clear message to their federation.

Sometimes the protest is about the kit itself. After the 2023 FIFA Women's World Cup, goalkeeper Mary Earps was the only English player who didn't have a replica jersey offered for sale by Nike, despite having been a major reason her squad made it to the finals. Even though she had to face off against a sports retail behemoth, Mary spoke up about this injustice, and fans quickly rallied behind her. No match for the wrath of the public, Nike released Mary's replica jersey, which immediately sold out. It was a win for often-overlooked female goalkeepers everywhere.

For the 2023 Women's World Cup, many nations stopped using white shorts after listening to player feedback. Wearing colored shorts helped reduce anxiety for female athletes and allowed them to focus on their sport when they were on their periods. Nike also incorporated leak protection technology in its kits. This small change went a long way in showing respect for female athletes and was a way to encourage more women to participate in sports.

England, Canada, France, Nigeria, and South Korea swapped out white shorts for colored ones for the first time during the 2023 FIFA Women's World Cup, adjusting for the realities of being a female athlete.

9

Game-Changers

The drive was supposed to be quick and unremarkable. With a police escort accompanying them, the women on the bus didn't anticipate any trouble getting to the stadium, but there they were, stuck in standstill traffic. The entire U.S. women's national soccer team now had a new layer of nerves on top of the many they were already trying to calm. They were about to compete in one of the most important games of their lives. One of the most important games in the whole sport's history—the 1999 FIFA Women's World Cup final. They had spent months training for this tournament, months hyping up the event to the public, and years dreaming of this chance to be world champions. Their first match, the cup's opener, was today and they needed to get to Giants Stadium—right now. How could there be this much traffic? The members of the team— including the hugely famous Mia Hamm, the respected veteran Michelle Akers, captain Carla Overbeck, goalkeeper Briana Scurry, and the outgoing Brandi Chastain—all pressed their faces against the bus windows to see what the holdup was.

What they saw shocked them. The cars were filled with girls, boys, and adults, their faces painted in red-white-and-blue, wearing their jerseys, holding American flags and homemade signs to support their team.

That's when it hit them. This traffic was all for them.

"Oh my god, this is really happening," midfielder Shannon MacMillan recalled thinking.

When the United States had initially won the bid to host the third FIFA Women's World Cup, the U.S. women's national team made an ambitious goal: to win the whole damn thing. But they also made another, even more lofty goal: to make this World Cup the biggest women's athletic event ever. They knew they had to succeed. The future of their sport depended on it. The next generation of female soccer players—the girls in the stands and at home, watching on television, were depending on them.

The tight-knit teammates looked at each other, elated, emotional, and filled with pride. Before even setting foot on the pitch, they felt a huge sense of victory.

It was just the boost they needed to launch them on their path to making history.

A Bigger, Bolder Vision

After inaugurating the 1991 FIFA Women's World Cup in Guangzhou in impressive fashion, the 1995 World Cup in Sweden had been a huge letdown. FIFA had only booked small stadiums and the biggest crowd during the whole tournament was a measly 5,000 fans. It was nothing compared to the 63,000 who had attended the final match four years before. For FIFA, the second Women's World Cup was a financial failure. This made female players across the globe very nervous. Since the beginning of its history, women's soccer was constantly fighting for its right to exist. After the invigorating glory of 1991, the lackluster 1995 tournament was a big step back. Would this cause FIFA to lose interest in women's soccer? An interest that was already flimsy to begin with? And would fans stick with them? Players were still aching for leagues, for paths to be professional athletes, to be better compensated for their talents—there was still so much growth needed. Without another successful World Cup, these goals would be unreachable.

The players' big dreams stayed afloat thanks to the 1996 Olympic Games in Atlanta, Georgia. Women's soccer had been included for the first time ever, and the stadiums had been packed, due to the many Americans who wanted to cheer on their home team, who ultimately won the gold.

With the wind on its back from its Olympic win, the U.S. was now hosting the third FIFA Women's World Cup. From the beginning, everyone underestimated the event and the athletes. FIFA was again insisting on smaller stadiums, believing the event could only match the meager fandom of Sweden's cup. But the American organizers had a bigger, bolder vision—*We can recreate the magic of the Atlanta Olympics*, they insisted to FIFA. *People will show up. Lots of them.*

They pitched all of the reasons why FIFA should let them book big American football stadiums:

Mia Hamm, 1998

- Americans loved large-scale athletic events.

- Women's soccer had continued to grow in the U.S., especially among kids.

- Soccer had grown even more popular, demonstrated by the launch of the men's league, Major League Soccer in 1996.

- Thanks to the Olympics, women's soccer now had a bona fide superstar in Mia Hamm.

- There was plenty of time to put forth an elaborate marketing campaign.

Along with many in the sporting world, FIFA was skeptical, but in the end, it was ultimately persuaded by the enthusiastic organizers (especially since the U.S. Soccer Federation agreed to foot part of the bill). The games were to be held in the larger stadiums across eight cities. The opener would be on the East Coast, in New Jersey's Giants Stadium, while the final would be held on the West Coast in the Rose Bowl stadium in Pasadena, California. Many thought FIFA was setting itself up for embarrassment. *This is a gamble that absolutely will not pay off*, they believed. People just didn't spend money on women's sports. The Olympics were an event with a special draw—there was no way as many people would buy tickets. Americans barely cared about soccer—the men's national team had just placed 32nd out of 32 teams in the last World Cup. Many were ready to witness a flop.

FIFA was only willing to give the organizers a budget of 30 million dollars, which was about ten percent of the budget of any Men's World Cup. In other words, FIFA valued the men's game about ten times more than the women's game. Undeterred, the organizers knew what they could accomplish with that money and maintained hope for their ambitious vision.

When the American players heard that the large stadiums had been booked, they were ecstatic. "Of course we can fill them!" was the shared belief among them.

They were used to being underestimated and no one believed in them more than they believed in themselves.

Together, they stood completely committed to making the 1999 Women's World Cup a success. They understood that in order for their sport to have a real future, they had to put in the work beyond the field. Just like the original hype women of women's soccer, Nettie Honeyball and Lady Florence Dixie, the U.S. national team players knew the key to their success was marketing and publicity.

Starting in 1997, the cup's organizers set up tents in Los Angeles and New York City, handing out bumper stickers featuring the official logo, which included a ponytailed player getting ready to kick a ball. Millions of brochures were sent out to fans, players, and coaches.

The U.S. players mobilized. They played friendly tournaments in the cup's soon-to-be host cities, they visited schools, sporting goods stores, clinics and camps, appeared at youth league tournaments and conventions, and all-star games and banquets. At all of these events, they mingled with young players and fans, handed out flyers, took photos, and signed autograph after autograph. *There's going to be a World Cup in Summer '99—can't wait to see you there*, they'd say every time. Hungry for female sports heroes, their fans loved them—and their ticket-buying parents did too. The U.S. women's national team players wowed on the field, and in every fan and media interaction, they showcased their trademark charm and charisma. They were just a lovable bunch.

> **They were the girls next door-type and represented what Americans loved in their sports athletes. They were accessible, tough, athletic, and committed, and win or lose exemplified a respectful attitude.**
>
> —Tony DiCicco,
> U.S. coach, 1994–1999

By the end of 1998, an extraordinary 200,000 tickets had already been sold. It seemed like the American organizers' predictions could be right—there were inklings that this cup was going to be a hit. There was no time to slow down, the players and the organizers pushed ahead with their intensive promotional campaigns.

Leading into the tournament, fan-favorite Mia Hamm appeared in a national commercial for the sports drink Gatorade with none other than one of the greatest and most famous male athletes of all time, basketball icon Michael Jordan. In the commercial, they competed against each other in various sports accompanied by the song "Anything You Can Do (I Can Do Better)." It was a glossy and cool commercial that went over really well with the millions who saw it. There was something so potent about seeing one of the best-known male athletes in the world go head-to-head with the best-known female athlete in the world.

It made girls and women feel proud and made boys and men pay attention.

In another super effective commercial, this time for Nike, four U.S. teammates in uniform were shown sitting in a dental office's waiting room. When they found out that their teammate Brandi Chastain required two fillings, in solidarity, one by one, the teammates each stood and pronounced, "I will have two fillings." The commercial ended with the inspired female receptionist also standing and asking for two fillings. This funny ad emphasized the team's committed bonds of sisterhood, their winning American spirit, and their good-natured and likable personalities.

In the era of broadcast television before streaming media, these two commercials were viewed by countless people who had never watched or previously cared about women's soccer. But now their interest was piqued. Before the tournament even started, the American public had become completely charmed by this fun-loving, appealing group of all-star athletes. The U.S. women's national team was on its way to becoming a sensation. Tickets were now selling fast.

Suddenly, they were everywhere in the American media. Defender Brandi Chastain, nicknamed "Hollywood" by her teammates due to her love of attention and flair for the dramatic, caused a stir by appearing in *Gear* magazine with strategically placed soccer balls covering her nude body. A few days before the tournament began, she appeared on the popular television show, *Late Night with David Letterman*. A breezy Brandi joked with host David Letterman, who called the team: "Babe City." Letterman's enthusiasm for the team became a running bit during the month-long cup.

Even though the media focused on the physical attractiveness of the players, Brandi and the rest of the U.S. squad were not offended. They saw it as an opportunity to show that athleticism and femininity could co-exist. For so long, soccer was deemed unwomanly, and now they were proving the opposite was true.

Soccer WAS womanly.

Women could care about their appearance and strive to be the best athletes in the world. The players embraced terms like "Babe City" as sources of empowerment, turning what could have been demeaning into something positive.

By the time the opening game finally arrived on June 19, 1999, Giants Stadium was completely sold out. The team and the cup had captured the attention of millions of Americans and beyond. It was now the moment to show everyone what they were really capable of—being fiercely competitive and superbly skilled world-class athletes. When the team's bus finally navigated through the highway traffic and pulled into the parking lot of Giants Stadium, the players were in for another surprise. The enormous parking lots were chock full of fans who had arrived early to participate in the great American sports tradition of tailgating—a pre-game party. Everywhere they looked, red-white-and-blue bedecked fans were cheerfully socializing, and girls and boys kicked around soccer balls. Number 9 Mia Hamm jerseys were everywhere. To the players, this was a beautiful sight. All of their hard work and hustle on and off the field had actually paid off. Just like the teammates always believed, it turned out people would buy tickets for women's sports.

That sold-out opening match between the United States and Denmark felt like a celebration of everything feminine. The seats had never been filled with so many young girls before—"ponytailed hooligans," as the press called them. For many of them, this was their first time seeing professional female athletes compete live. This was the largest crowd for a women's sports event in America. Everywhere they looked, girlhood was being saluted. The stadium was adorned with banners featuring the tournament's slogan:

This is My Game. This is My Future. Watch Me Play.

As an extra treat, organizers had chosen boy band *NSYNC to perform during the half-time show.

When the Danish and American teams ran through the players' tunnels and onto the field, they were greeted by the smell of fresh-cut grass, thousands of flashing cameras, and 77,000 fans going bonkers. Yellow logo-adorned thunder sticks had been handed out to fans and their *thump thump thump* added to the uproar.

Although there were Danish fans present wearing their red and white, the crowd was mostly made of the host team's fans who broke out into a thunderous chant: "U.S.A., U.S.A., U.S.A.!"

The players had never experienced anything like this before. "I know it gave me goosebumps. How could [it] not?" Mia Hamm remembered.

In that first match, the U.S. commanded the field and rewarded their fans by beating Denmark 3-0 thanks to goals by Mia Hamm, Julie Foudy, and Kristine Lilly. Kicking off the tournament with a win by the host nation was important. The team knew they had to keep winning in order to keep selling tickets and to maintain their newly minted American fans' attention. Yes, they were hungry for a championship, for this cup, but they were even hungrier for the bigger prizes a successful cup would bring the whole sport and future generations.

From there, the tournament continued, and across the country, the matches between the sixteen participating nations were played before packed crowds. Stands couldn't keep merchandise stocked. And millions watched them on television too. Unlike the prior two World Cups, every single game was being broadcast to the American people. For three weeks, the Women's World Cup was front-page news in the U.S.—a national obsession. The joyous atmosphere and celebration of feminism continued.

Much to their fans' delight, the United States dominated their games. They earned their way out of the group stage by crushing Nigeria 7-1, then beat North Korea in the quarter finals, followed by Brazil in the semi-finals.

Even though the team was made up of exceptional individual players, coach Tony DiCicco played a pivotal role in the team's success. He unlocked the secret to getting the best out of them after Mia Hamm gave him feedback early on in his tenure:

"Coach us like men, but treat us like women."

Physically, he trained them as hard as any men's team. They could handle it, no question. But emotionally, he adapted his methods. He stopped yelling so much, emphasized positive reinforcement, provided emotional support, and encouraged their camaraderie. This approach was appreciated by the players, and it showed on the field. And now this team was headed to a World Cup final.

The U.S. was to face China. Many considered China the technically superior team. They were faster, played a better possession game, and had their own lethal weapon in superstar scoring machine, Sun Wen. The U.S. knew that the championship wasn't going to be handed to them. They would have to play their best to win. But they also knew they had two advantages over China. First, they were playing on their home turf and second, they knew how to be world champs—they had already done it twice before.

A Hard-Fought Match

July 10, 1999 was a steaming hot day in Pasadena, California. When the Chinese and U.S. teams emerged from the players' tunnels and arrived on the pitch in front of 90,185 people, it was an unbelievable sight. "There was this explosion of fan noise and it sucked the air out of me. I was like 'Oh my god, I'd never seen so many people,'" recalled Shannon MacMillan. In the crowd, the U.S. team had their friends and families, including the children of the two moms on the team, Joy Fawcett and Carla Overbeck.

Hall of Fame:
Sun Wen

Sun Wen was introduced to football by her dad and became one of women's soccer's first superstars. She played in the very first Women's World Cup in Guangzhou as a teenager and earned both the Golden Ball and Golden Boot awards. With 106 international goals, Sun is China's all-time highest goal scorer. She was known not only for her ability to score, but also for her speed, precision in passing, and energetic personality. Since retiring, she's put her leadership skills and love of football to good use by helping grow China's women's football program. In 2000, Sun was named the FIFA Women's Player of the Century along with Michelle Akers.

Also in attendance was President of the United States, Bill Clinton, sitting with First Lady Hillary Clinton and their teenage daughter, Chelsea, along with a host of celebrities like Oprah Winfrey, Tom Hanks, Halle Berry, Courteney Cox, and Drew Barrymore. An astonishing forty million people watched from home in the U.S.

During the U.S. national anthem—sung by boy band, Hanson—four F-Fighter jets flew overhead, startling the Chinese players. The sight was meant to be a visual spectacle, but it also had the effect of reinforcing the power of the U.S. team. The Chinese team was exceptional, but this was going to be a hard-fought match.

The two teams were clearly tense, and neither team performed to the best of their abilities. The first two halves produced a scoreless game. Now that the regulation ninety minutes had run out, they would go into "sudden death" extra time, with the nerve-wracking Golden Goal rule in effect. In sudden death, the teams played up to thirty minutes of extra time. Whichever team scored a goal first—the Golden Goal—would be declared the winner.

From the players, to the coaches, to the crowd, to the television viewers—everyone was on the edge of their seats.

Ten minutes into sudden death, China's Lui Ailing launched a perfect corner kick in front of the U.S. goal, where Fan Yunjie expertly nailed it with her head. The crowd gasped and cringed as the ball flew just past goalkeeper Briana Scurry's fingertips toward the goal. But waiting right behind Briana—exactly where she was supposed to be—was her teammate, Kristine Lilly, who blasted the ball away with her head. From the middle of a trio of Chinese players, Brandi Chastain then cleared it upfield and away from the danger zone. Those terrifying milliseconds could have ended the game tragically for the U.S.

Shaken, but still determined, the Americans were able to keep China away from the goal for the remainder of the sudden death round. When the whistle blew, the players on both squads were completely drained from playing 120 minutes of World Cup final soccer. The only thing worse than the Golden Goal rule was what they had to face next. Now the game was to be decided by dreaded penalty kicks.

The teams chose five players apiece who would each take a single shot from the center of the penalty box. It's shooter versus goalkeeper during penalty kicks, and the shooter is heavily favored, most scoring unless they make a mistake or the goalie manages an awesome save. In the U.S. goal was a laser-focused Briana Scurry, who had played incredibly well the entire World Cup. Equally fearsome was China's Gao Hong. When it came to shooters, the U.S. was already short their best penalty kicker, Michelle Akers. She had battled injuries and a brutal case of chronic fatigue syndrome and had to be scraped off the field in the last minute of regular time. Coach DiCicco put Mia Hamm on the list. She was fantastic at scoring goals during the match, but she was not a confident penalty kicker. Mia thought Shannon MacMillan was a better choice, but when she proposed it, assistant coach, Lauren Gregg, told her the list had already been submitted. Mia would take the kick. Also on the list was Brandi Chastain who, unlike Mia, was utterly confident in her ability to put this ball in the back of the net.

Hall of Fame:
Briana Scurry

Briana Scurry's parents put her in goal as a young girl, thinking it was the safest position for her on an all-boys soccer team. Little did they know that Briana would grow up to become one of the best female goalkeepers to ever play the game. When Briana faced the Chinese players during the famous 1999 World Cup shootout, she was not only one of two Black players, she was also the only openly lesbian player on the team. Bold Briana inspired so many young girls to pursue their own dreams. Her career ended abruptly in 2010 after a severe concussion on the field. Despite suffering a traumatic brain injury resulting in depression and anxiety, this experience led Briana to become a coach, broadcaster, and an advocate for mental health and the LGBTQ+ community. She was inducted into the U.S. National Women's Hall of Fame in 2017.

Even after Coach DiCicco gave her the instruction: "Use your left foot." Brandi was a righty but had a strong left foot. Using it might throw off the goalie. *Left it is*, Brandi immediately accepted.

With a captivated, anxious, breath-holding audience of 90,000 fans, the goalkeepers took their positions. The ten shooters gathered at midfield. The championship rested entirely on the next few moments.

One by one, the first shooters proceeded to the penalty spot and took their kicks.

Xie Huilin. In.
Carla Overbeck. In.
Qiu Haiyan. In.
Joy Fawcett. In.

When Liu Ying fired away, Briana dove left and blocked the shot.

The crowd and her teammates went nuts. Adrenaline rushed through her and she pumped her arms and banged on her chest for the crowd. Ying leaned her head back, crushed by her failure.

Now it was absolutely crucial for the remaining U.S. team members to score. If they did, they would be world champions. The pressure was enormous.

Next up, Kristine Lilly. In.
Zhang Ouying. In.
Mia Hamm. In. (Despite her nerves.)
Sun Wen. In. (Of course.)

Finally, it was all up to Brandi Chastain. If she missed, the penalty kicks would go on, and her team risked losing the world championship on what felt like a coin flip.

But if she made the shot, the cup was theirs.

In training, Brandi had practiced penalty kicks religiously. She had also played out this kind of glory moment in her mind over and over again. This was "Hollywood," after all, and she dreamed of playing a hero's role in a great sports victory.

Brandi knew what she had to do. The crowd was nearly silent as she placed the ball, backed away and then drove it toward the goal. The second the ball hit the back of the net, the crowd erupted and the U.S. became the 1999 FIFA Women's World Cup champions.

In a moment she later called "temporary insanity," Brandi immediately dropped down to her knees, and in a move replicating her male soccer heroes, ripped off her jersey, unveiling her strong body and a black Nike sports bra. It was an image of power and triumph.

The entire team sprinted toward Brandi, jumped into each other's arms, embracing each other with joy. The crowd went wild, as did many of the 40 million fans watching from their television screens. A devastated Chinese team looked on, their heads down.

A Win for Women Everywhere

The celebrations had only just begun. For weeks following their epic win, the U.S. women's national team was feted across the country—a blizzard of interviews, magazine photo shoots, an appearance on the *Late Show with David Letterman*, sports game appearances, a ticker-tape parade in New York City, Wheaties cereal boxes with their images plastered on them, a NASA shuttle launch invitation, and even a trip to the White House. Everywhere, fans lined up for autographs and photos, which the players were always game to provide.

What the Americans had accomplished was the highest high in women's soccer so far. There had been bright spots before—Dick, Kerr, the 1971 cup in Mexico, that first FIFA World Cup in 1991—but this time, it seemed that the sport had really, truly, and finally been embraced by the public at large. This team had shattered the stubborn beliefs that women's soccer wasn't a moneymaker and it wasn't worth fully developing or paying attention to.

There was a certain magic to this particular group of women. Not only were they an amazing soccer team, but they were also friendly, earnest, spirited athletes who inspired everyone around them. They were unified in their belief that what they were doing was important, not just for them—but for the generations born after them.

> ## Many girls saw themselves in these athletes—an experience they'd never had before.

After watching the U.S. team win the cup, multitudes of girls went out and kicked around a soccer ball—some for the first time, and others with the new resolution to be the next Mia Hamm. Women's soccer wasn't only being normalized for women— two-thirds of the cup's television viewership had been male. And all of this was true not just in the United States, but around the world. Countries that had never really thought much about their women's soccer programs now decided to pour money into developing them. They wanted a piece of this feel-good glory too.

> ## *The 1999 U.S. women's soccer team had captured lightning in a bottle, and they had done it their way.*

They inspired their coach to coach them their way. They publicized the tournament their way. They played their way. They had celebrated female athleticism, female camaraderie, female bodies, and female competitiveness. And by doing so, they changed the course of women's soccer history forever, which was a win in many ways for women everywhere.

" This is more than a game. It's about female athletes. It's about sports. It's about everything. "

–Kristine Lilly,
U.S. midfielder and forward, 1987–2010

● ● ●

Global Game: South Korea

Women's soccer in South Korea started growing in the 1940s, but it took off after the 1999 Women's World Cup. Inspired by the event, the Korean government funded the development of the sport at all levels, and amazingly, South Korea qualified for its first Women's World Cup just four years later. Today, Korea remains a strong presence in women's soccer, producing top-level talent like Ji So-yun, the all-time top goal scorer for the Taegeuk Ladies.

10

A League of Their Own

After the colossal success of the 1999 FIFA Women's World Cup, it seemed like women's soccer would finally get the financial support and fandom it needed to fully blossom. For three weeks, millions around the world were enchanted by the sport and its players—surely the love affair with women's soccer had just begun? Well, if you've been reading this book, you already know that nothing ever comes easily for women's soccer and its players. It's one step forward, three steps back, all along the way.

The '99 Cup had achieved a lot in showing the world that women's soccer was entertaining, money-making, had incredible athletes, and edge-of-your-seat matches. It also provided many little girls with their own female athletic heroes for the very first time. The importance of this was something that hadn't ever crossed many people's minds before, and now they had seen how powerful it was. But there were still more goals to achieve.

The players dreamed of a real professional league.

So far in its entire history, in America or anywhere else, women's soccer had never had a true pro league. One where players were paid a salary so that playing soccer could be their job, not just a hobby. National team players wanted to be able to focus wholly on soccer and not have to work a side hustle on top of training, traveling, promoting, and playing matches. And beyond them, players who didn't make their national teams longed for a place to continue to play at an elite level. At that time, countries like Sweden, Germany, and Japan had semi-pro leagues, but players couldn't live off what they were paid.

Of course, men's pro leagues existed very early in the sport's history. And by 2000, men's leagues around the world were thriving, with top players getting huge endorsement deals and making jaw-dropping multimillion-dollar salaries. Meanwhile, the best female soccer athletes in the world had spent most—if not all—of their careers playing for free or for next to nothing. Only recently had female players started to get endorsement deals, but that was a privilege reserved for superstars like Mia Hamm and a few others. The female footballers weren't in it for the money, but it sure would be nice to make enough to survive as a pro athlete, an opportunity that had already been afforded to men for over a century.

A pro league also offered the opportunity to up everyone's game and to push the development of their sport forward. With a league, they had more opportunities to train and compete. Every player would become a better and more competitive athlete. "It's imperative that a league happen for women's soccer to continue to compete at this level," U.S. national team defender Joy Fawcett expressed at the time.

Women's soccer had come so far, but for it to have a real future, launching a professional league was completely critical.

First Shot: The Women's United Soccer Association

Now that they were stars, the members of the U.S. national team knew if there was ever a moment to launch a league, this was it. They mobilized and put pressure on the important stakeholders, unified in their message:

It's time for a league, let's make it happen.

America's Major League Soccer had begun efforts to put together a secondary women's league, but female footballers were only lukewarm to that particular plan. They were wary of being tethered to an organization that openly valued the men's sport more and was struggling to be successful to begin with. The women's national team was already way more popular and more successful than the U.S. men's national team—they wanted a league of their own.

In February 2000, less than a year after the epic World Cup shoot-out finale, a big announcement was made. A group of eight media industry executives had come together and pledged 40 million dollars to create the very first professional women's soccer league in the world, the Women's United Soccer Association, to be known as the WUSA.

For the players, it was the "pinch me" moment they had long dreamed of. And the joy wasn't contained only to the United States. The WUSA would be open to international talent too, meaning the best of the best of female soccer players around the world would be showcased. Finally, this was the league they knew they deserved.

"We have dreamt [. . .] about this day since we were born . . . and talked about it and fantasized about it and have said how cool would it be to not only start a league in this country where women can play professional soccer, [. . .] but to have the best league in the entire world." Julie Foudy excitedly expressed at a press conference.

WUSA founding players Mia Hamm and Julie Foudy.

From the moment of its creation, the WUSA rode the coattails of the U.S. women's national soccer team's fame. Mia Hamm was the league's shiniest star, but the entire '99 squad had become national celebrities. All twenty world champs were offered spots in the league, spread across the eight inaugural teams. Not only that, they were also each given a financial stake in the league as founding players. It was clear that the WUSA was relying on these players' popularity to draw their adoring fans to the games, many of whom were young girls.

When it came to money, players were to be paid a minimum of $27,000, with a maximum of $85,000. This was not a huge amount of money, even by 2000 standards. It was also less than the MLS players received and didn't even compare to some players' salaries in the elite European and South American leagues. They might not have had the ability to buy a fancy new car, but it was enough for the female footballers to actually get to play the sport they loved for a living.

Birgit Prinz of Germany was one of the WUSA's prized international recruits, playing for the Carolina Courage.

With the U.S. national team players spread out across the country, the rest of the team rosters were filled with former ace college players and top international players, including China's Sun Wen and Gao Hong and European stars like Norway's Hege Riise, Germany's Birgit Prinz, and France's Marinette Pichon. For many, this was the first time they had competed outside their own national team. Now they were on the same team as players from other countries and cultures, who had different styles, personalities, and spoke different languages. It was something to adapt to, but something they could all benefit from. The potential to improve the state of women's soccer was thrilling.

Everything about this opportunity was thrilling.

> **I still can't believe it. On the first day of practice, just walking into the locker room and seeing the [...] practice gear, to know it was there for us, it's unbelievable. It's a dream come true. There's no other way to put it.**

–Keri Sarver,
Washington Freedom forward, 2001

The very first professional women's league match was held in Washington, D.C.'s RFK Stadium on April 14, 2001. The matchup was between the Washington Freedom and the Bay Area CyberRays. East Coast versus West Coast. Mia Hamm's team versus Brandi Chastain's team. The WUSA wasn't subtle about pushing the fame of the two most famous female players—banners outside the stadium and ads emblazoned on city buses read:

MIA vs BRANDI
Washington Freedom   **Bay Area CyberRays**

For that first match, the league flew out all of the founding players. Legendary tennis player Billie Jean King did the coin toss. Also in attendance were other groundbreaking athletes like the captain of the 1991 World Cup championship team, April Heinrichs, and members of the Ladies Professional Golf Association. At that first match, the stadium was filled with 34,000 fans, half of which were young and teenage girls. Like the '99 World Cup, it was family-friendly and had a celebratory atmosphere. The opening ceremony included fireworks and female parachutists. Hundreds of girls lined up to get the players' autographs and treated them like pop stars. It was an awesome start for the league. The players felt immensely proud and excited.

Coming off the back of the 1999 World Cup craziness, and now kicking off with this new league, surrounded by the greatest female football talent in the world, the future felt so bright.

The World Cup final had attracted 40 million viewers. Five-hundred thousand tickets had been sold to the tournament. More than 60,000 fans had attended the final match. The big question now was: would fans come out in droves to support the WUSA? Unfortunately, they didn't. At all.

The launch of the WUSA was splashy, making national headlines. The league knew that it was unrealistic to expect the same level of success as the World Cup, but surely they could capture a meaningful portion of that fandom. But in the league's first year, it only attracted an average of 8,000 fans per game. The second year was even worse, attracting less than 7,000 fans per game. The biggest and most disappointing surprise was that barely anyone was watching the games on television. By the second year, the cable station that had agreed to show all the games had backed out after being scared away by the low ratings, and then it became difficult for fans to figure out how to even watch the games. Viewership plummeted. An estimated $100 million was poured into the league by investors. But everyone involved was losing money. With such low turnout and viewership, the league couldn't get the corporate sponsors they desperately needed. Founder John Hendricks bemoaned the situation: "Every time I see a deal with a male athlete for a shoe for five . . . ten million dollars, I say, 'Goodness, why don't you invest in 160 players and an international league and all these fans?'" The players were frustrated too at the lack of interest in sponsoring the women's league. "It's not much money," Julie Foudy pointed out. "Here you had this special product that was a unique sporting experience for kids and families. It's such a great demographic. That's the heartbreaker. It's [. . .] a sad reflection on society."

Sports leagues are a business, and this was a business that wasn't making any money. Actually, it was losing tons of money. Even though the league hoped to get a boost from the 2003 World Cup, it was in such a bad state, it couldn't even scrape by until the event. After just three years, the WUSA went out of business. The heartbreaking announcement was made only five days before the 2003 Women's World Cup.

The players were devastated. Their dream was shattered.

What a terrible way to go into the World Cup. And their loyal, if small, group of fans was also heartbroken. Some even offered to have a bake sale to help. But the WUSA was officially dead.

So why didn't the WUSA work out?

- One of the biggest reasons was purely business—everyone spent too much money. The league had a lavish and flashy rollout, but costs were underestimated and fan interest overestimated. The league was bleeding money and not coming close to making any.

- Another criticism was that the people in charge were media industry people, not soccer people.

- And the marketing and promotion hadn't been quite right—the league had targeted tween girls and soccer moms, but older girls and their sports-loving, ticket-buying dads would have been a better choice. Being a Mia Hamm superfan seemed cool for tween girls—but then they seemed to age out of it. The league needed to convince older kids and teenagers that women's soccer was for them too.

- They had also perhaps placed too much emphasis on the '99 players. The fans loved a handful of players but they weren't necessarily invested in the teams themselves.

- Most disappointingly, it seemed that even after the success of the World Cup, people weren't ready to embrace women's sports in a continuous way. A one-off event like the World Cup was exciting, but a league required fans to keep showing up.

If the players and organizers got another shot at a league, they would have to fix these mistakes.

Second Attempt: Women's Professional Soccer

Although the collapse of the WUSA was utterly heart-wrenching, many of its players didn't give up hope. It still felt like the right time in history for a women's league. Another World Cup and another Olympics were on the horizon where new, young stars would emerge and draw in fans. They believed it wasn't the end—and they weren't wrong. In September 2007, only a year after the WUSA had folded, a new announcement was made: women's soccer was being given a second chance at a professional league. It would be called WPS, short for Women's Professional Soccer. Eager to learn from the mistakes of the WUSA, WPS was structured differently.

This time, the league didn't own all the teams. Instead, the teams were individually owned, and the league was its own separate, governing entity. This would help the league reel in spending, while the owners of the teams managed their own money. There was also a new approach to marketing. WPS still loved their tween girl fans, but they were going to try to appeal beyond them. The goal was for the teams in the league to build followings and fandoms made up of all kinds of soccer fans.

Overall, WPS relied less on the star power of its players in the hopes that fans would form an attachment to teams, not just individual players. But they knew attracting amazing players was also key to the league's success. Like the WUSA, WPS was filled with U.S. national team players—with many from the famous '99 squad—but now they also had new stars from the 2003 team, including striker Abby Wambach. While the league wasn't quite as stacked with expensive international stars as before, it did manage to attract a glittering gem of a player all the way from Brazil: Marta Vieira da Silva, known simply as Marta. She would become known as one of the best to ever play the game. Although professional club teams and leagues in other countries had started to develop, international players still saw WPS as a unique opportunity to make soccer their career. England's star Kelly Smith came to the U.S. to play for the Boston Breakers because "at home, most people treat [women's soccer] as a joke."

Abby Wambach, 2007

Coming off the failure of the WUSA, the bar was lowered for everything. There were fewer teams: seven instead of eight. Each team had fewer players and they were paid lower salaries. The stadiums were smaller. Although it was disappointing to take such a step back, the players just felt grateful for this second chance.

They believed in themselves and were hopeful for the future.

They just needed to show that a women's soccer league could be successful and then everything would improve.

From the beginning, WPS was treated more like a startup company. The money for big promo campaigns was gone, but by 2007, social media sites Facebook and Twitter had become popular and provided a whole new way to connect with fans. WPS was an early adopter and was one of the first sports leagues to fully embrace social media. It not only used it to deliver news and promote the league, but it also encouraged the players to actively tweet.

Alex Scott ✅
@Boston Breakers, 2009-2011

Still hurting from getting beat 4-0, a game to forget, good goal Karen, will see you for a rematch soon, hehe.

Karen Carney ✅
@Chicago Red Stars, 2009-2010

On my way to training . . . no game this week = running

Tweets like these may seem pretty mundane now, but at the time, Twitter was brand new and getting this intimate window into a pro athlete's life was really exciting. The league even encouraged bench players to tweet from the sidelines during matches. So would this fresh approach and these innovative new tactics work out for WPS?

Sadly, the answer was no. WPS was launched in a fragile state and was never able to grow strong. Attendance was still low—even lower than before. Teams kept losing tons of money and closing down:

- Los Angeles Sol was the first year's champ—and then it folded.

- FC Gold Pride was the second year's champ—and then it folded.

- Another team, magicJack, had been terminated by WPS for not following league rules.

- By the end of the third year, after lots of reshuffling, the league only had five teams, and risked losing its status as a pro league. Their biggest corporate sponsor, athletic brand Puma, pulled out.

- To make things worse, the league became embroiled in a legal battle with the owner of magicJack.

The league was in a complete state of disarray. Despite a much-needed boost in attendance thanks to the 2007 World Cup, all of its problems were too much to overcome. Just like the WUSA, WPS was shut down after three years.

In less than a decade, two professional women's soccer leagues in the U.S. had failed. The idea of a pro women's soccer league had become a joke. Their failed attempts had only succeeded in fueling the fire of the naysayers who said women's sports couldn't ever be successful. It was such a disappointment. Most players believed there was no way that they would get a third chance at a league. They had invested so much in training and competing, building strong bonds with their teammates, and connecting with their loving fans, and it was all gone. Again. Many decided to retire from pro soccer for good—a whole generation of potential game-changers disappeared. Others returned to amateur and semi-pro leagues, and that would have to be enough for them.

A small group still held on to a glimmer of hope that perhaps the dream of a league was not entirely dead, that maybe the league was still finding its way.

Hall of Fame
Marta

When Marta was growing up in 1990s Brazil, she'd wad up grocery bags in the shape of a ball, desperate for any opportunity to play her beloved sport. Despite major disapproval by her family, Marta's truth was undeniable: she was better than all the boys. She was so good that she was benched because the coaches didn't want to embarrass the boys. Marta always found a way to play and to wow. She went on to have a brilliant career as a striker, playing for clubs abroad, including in the United States, and for the Brazilian national team. She led her team in six World Cups and six Olympic Games. She scored seventeen World Cup goals, setting the record for any footballer—man or woman. She was named FIFA World Player of the Year six times. Marta's control of the ball was incredible to see, her little flicks and tricks getting the best of hundreds—maybe thousands—of opponents. No one could dribble as fast as Marta, and her ability to score goals was always feared. Her insane skills earned her the right to wear Brazil's sacred #10 on her yellow jersey—the same number as the great Pelé. An icon at home in Brazil and around the world, Marta was able to influence the development of her sport in Brazil, which had suffered for years due to a strict ban. She also lived openly as a lesbian woman, and has been embraced by the LGBTQ+ community as a beloved heroine. In 2024, soccer fans were delighted when she became engaged to her Orlando Pride teammate, Carrie Lawrence. Without a doubt, Marta is the greatest female footballer of all time.

11

Last Chance:
The National Women's Soccer League

A third chance at a league? To many, there was no way that was going to happen. *People just don't care enough about women's soccer*, was now the common belief. But as soon as WPS shut down, a group of believers, including representatives from the national team, were figuring out how to move forward yet again. This passionate group held on to the conviction that the league just needed to find its right form. *How can we get it right this time?* was the tough question they debated. Against all odds, in December 2012, a new, third league was announced, the National Women's Soccer League, or the NWSL.

Third time's a charm, right?

Everyone knew this was truly their last chance. There had to be a whole new approach, one that learned from all of the previous mistakes. Although some teams from the WPS were carried over into the new league, and many of the players returned, the NWSL was going to be different. It was going to be well-run, on budget, draw sponsors consistently, and develop a strong fan base.

Failure was not an option.

This time, the biggest difference was that the U.S. Soccer Federation was involved. The federation knew that if the United States was going to continue its dominance in women's soccer, it absolutely needed its own pro league. The American squad was still considered the best team in the world, but the gap between them and everyone else was getting smaller. Other countries were catching up. England had launched its Women's Super League and strong clubs like France's *Olympique Lyonnais Féminin* had emerged in Europe, attracting talent from around the world. Without a league for American women to regularly play, train, and compete for spots on the national team, the U.S. risked losing its position at the top. As the governing body for all pro soccer in the country, the federation wasn't going to let that happen.

Everyone entered into the new league humbled by an entire decade of defeat. Even the players were skeptical. "Honestly, it's happened [twice]," Abby Wambach told journalists when they asked her if she thought the NWSL would work out. "It's risen and fallen two times. Those two times I was wrong." National team members had started looking abroad for opportunities to up their game and needed to be convinced that this time, a league was sustainable.

But the players were intrigued by the smart, new structure of the NWSL. The federations of the United States, Mexico, and Canada would finance the salaries of their own national team players, and the individual teams could pay for the other players from their modest funds. This way, the federations felt good about their top players getting the exposure they needed to compete at the highest level, and the leagues had a better shot at staying afloat financially.

One downside to this being the third attempt at a league was that salary expectations were the lowest they'd ever been. Some players in the NWSL made a pitiful $6,000 a year, the minimum salary. This was a big drop from the $27,000 minimum promised ten years before in the WUSA. It wasn't even a livable wage. But by this time, the players were just desperate to have a league to play in, so they accepted the suboptimal situation, and hoped things would improve as the league proved itself.

Salaries weren't the only downgrade. With more realistic expectations in mind, the teams played in smaller college or municipal stadiums, some even playing in high school stadiums. And instead of a major corporate sponsor like Puma, the league

The Portland Thorns were one of the NWSL's first successful teams, both financially and athletically.

drew smaller sponsors like a family-run meatpacking company. The attitude at the time was: *We'll take what we can get.*

The NWSL launched without the glitz and glamour of the WUSA's opening, but there was joy and optimism. Instead of relying on a traditional television broadcaster, the league streamed its games live on the internet so that fans could easily watch. This careful approach was enough to keep the NWSL stable for its first few years. In 2015, it got a big boost from the Women's World Cup, after the U.S. won the tournament. The U.S. women's national team had once again captured the hearts of many Americans. New fans were created and old fans were reminded of how much they liked this team. The hope was that national team fans would show up to a NWSL game, have a good time, and sense how special the league was—and then buy tickets to more games. As Arnim Whisler, the owner of the Chicago Red Stars, put it, "Once you've been here a couple times, you really want to be a part of it."

From the launch of the NWSL, one team seemed to have figured out the formula to success: the Portland Thorns, which was associated with the men's pro team, the Portland Timbers.

The strategy was simple—treat the women's team just like the men's team.

The Thorns used the same staff as the Timbers, their logo was displayed in the same size as the Timbers' logo at the office, the hype for the team was the same, they would play in the same stadium. And it worked. From the beginning, many Timbers fans became Thorns fans. The Thorns put butts in seats like no other women's pro league team had ever done before. What a revelation it was: *Hmm, maybe taking the women's team as seriously as the men's team is the key to success.* And the Thorns played nice—its leadership agreed to share some of their profits with the whole league and also revealed the details of their tactics so that other NWSL teams could attempt to recreate the magic.

Every couple of years, the NWSL would reach a new notch of success—better broadcast deals and better sponsors which led to higher salaries and more amenities for the players, and even bigger stadiums and expansion teams. The longer the league was in existence, the more skilled the players became. The more top international talent it attracted, the better the quality of play and the more exciting the matches. Fandoms grew. Progress was slow, but it was steady.

All the while, the players held their breath. Outside of playing soccer, they knew the next most important part of their jobs was to change people's minds about the league. They put up with a lot, especially those first years—some teams didn't have on-site showers in their locker rooms, dedicated training rooms, or equipment managers. No one wanted to hurt the league, so no one spoke up at first, but as the league showed signs of being healthy, members of the national team acted as representatives and pushed for better conditions. It wasn't until ten years into the existence of the NWSL that the players finally let out that long-held breath:

The league was sustainable and wasn't going anywhere.

A big turning point occurred in 2020 when a new expansion team came to Los Angeles, Angel City FC. For the first time ever, a pro sports team was owned by a group of mostly female investors. And not just any investors, but celebrity

Angel City FC goalkeeper Dijana Haracic during a NWSL match.

investors like actress Natalie Portman, former national team players like Mia Hamm, Abby Wambach, and Julie Foudy, tennis legends Billie Jean King and Serena Williams, and her investor husband Alexis Ohanian. The team was cool and flashy, immediately making headlines and drawing fans. Its leadership treated it like a winning team—and a winning business—from the start. The strategy worked.

Angel City FC regularly attracted nearly 20,000 fans for every match, proving again that if a pro women's team is handled like a first-rate sports venture, it can succeed.

By the 2020s, the NWSL had expanded from its original eight to fourteen teams. Angel City's success inspired other celebrity investors to get involved. National team players Brandi Chastain, Briana Scurry, and Carli Lloyd, the National Football League's Patrick Mahomes and tennis's Naomi Osaka all invested in NWSL teams. These investors went a long way in adding credibility to the league and piquing the interest of new fans. Big corporate sponsors like Nike, Amazon, Google, EA Sports, and Delta Airlines signaled that this league was right up there with the other U.S. pro leagues.

Unlike its predecessors, the NWSL succeeded in drawing soccer fans of all ages and all walks of life. But the league never forgot who its core fandom was. It still has the youngest fan demographic in all of professional sports in the United States. Unlike any other pro league in America, it caters to its young female fans. Like when Angel City's Alyssa Thompson, the first NWSL player to get recruited out of high school, had to miss her senior prom because of a match, Angel City organized a "prom night" where Alyssa got to wear her dress, teammates got dressed up in their finest attire before the match, and fans held up signs saying:

In 2023, the league sold 1.2 million tickets to its games and pulled in over 800,000 viewers for its championship game. By that time, the league didn't rely on the federations' money anymore to help sustain the league.

It was official: the NWSL was a full-fledged success.

It took three attempts and about twenty years, but finally a professional women's soccer league was here to stay. Any doubts that the sport couldn't draw fans or that people "didn't care about women's soccer" were finally obliterated. And this wasn't just true in the United States—club teams and leagues across the world developed large, loving fandoms. Since the incredible 1999 World Cup finale, female footballers never gave up on the dream of a pro league. They fought for one privilege at a time, proving themselves again and again. And with each new privilege, the players set their sights on the next goal. Now that they were in this new, exciting era, it was time for their boldest goal yet—one that was utterly unimaginable generations ago.

This time, their goal was financial equality.

Beyond the Pitch

 ### **Bend It Like Beckham**

In 2002, the movie *Bend it Like Beckham* hit theaters and surprised everyone. In the movie, teenager Jess is football-obsessed, but her conservative Indian Punjabi family doesn't approve of her playing. Jess joins a women's team anyway, finding friendship and love along the way, eventually coming face-to-face with her parents' expectations. In addition to being a heartfelt cultural story that allowed many to see themselves reflected on the screen for the first time, the movie was a fun celebration of women's soccer and female athleticism.

12

The Ultimate Goal—Equality

Ninety-five days before a World Cup, the players on a national team are usually focused on training hard, staying in peak physical shape, competing for a spot on the final roster, studying other teams, and cementing bonds with teammates, all with the goal of becoming world champions. In 2019, U.S. players Megan Rapinoe, Carli Lloyd, Alex Morgan, and their teammates wanted to fully concentrate on winning. But they couldn't.

The U.S. women's soccer team had to also aim for a much bigger victory: fighting for equality for women and shattering a long-standing unjust system.

With three months to go before the Women's World Cup, on March 8, 2019—International Women's Day—twenty-eight members of the women's national team filed a lawsuit against their federation, U.S. Soccer. Their qualm with their employer? Gender discrimination. They were paid less than the men's team for the same work, and they were provided with inferior working conditions. It was unfair and against the law. In their thunderous lawsuit, the athletes demanded an end to this unfair treatment, as well as 67 million dollars in back pay and compensation.

This wasn't the first time the women's national team had pushed hard for fairer payment and better working conditions. The first time was in 1996 when Julie Foudy, inspired by a conversation with tennis champion Billie Jean King about her own fight for equal pay in the 1970s, led a lockout with eight other teammates. They refused to play until the federation agreed to offer them better compensation for the upcoming Olympic Games. Over the years, the players consistently pushed the federation to recognize their worth, as they were tired of staying in roach motels, earning just $10 a day, sitting in middle seats of smoking sections on airplanes, and having to resort to taking hotel shuttles to games—all while it seemed like the red carpet was being rolled out for the men's team.

> **We used to label it as 'character building' in the beginning. And then you start to get to a point where you're like, 'Okay, we're full of character now. We're overflowing with character. Let's move on this.'**
>
> —Julie Foudy,
> U.S. midfielder, 1988–2004

Back then, the women's team did not hold that much power. They were a fledgling team in a fledgling sport. But now, things were different. The U.S. women's national team was a much bigger beast. By 2019, they were the best women's soccer team in the world. Since 1991, they had won three World Cups and four gold medals at the Olympics. They had been ranked number one by FIFA for ten of the previous eleven years. More than 25 million viewers had watched the U.S. play in the World Cup final against Japan. And they generated tons and tons of money for their federation.

Despite being a record-breaking powerhouse, there was a big difference in how they were paid compared to the men's national team. Consider the numbers, in 2019:

- If the men's team played twenty exhibition matches a year, the players would earn an average of about $263,320 each.

- Meanwhile, for the same number of matches, members of the women's team earned a maximum of $99,000.

- In the 2014 World Cup, the men's team didn't even make it out of the first round, but U.S. Soccer paid 5.7 million dollars in bonuses to the men's team.

- In the 2015 World Cup, the women won the whole damn thing, and the players split only 1.7 million dollars.

So for the exact same work, the women were systematically paid less than the men.

Seriously?

Beyond finances, the women also faced worse working conditions, being forced to play on artificial turf thirteen times in a three-year period, which is known to increase the risk of injury compared to real grass. During this same period, the male players were only forced to play on turf once.

For the exact same work, the women were subject to worse, more dangerous conditions than the men. Just because of their gender. Oh, and by "same work," the women actually did the work much, much better. They were champions multiple times over, and the American men, simply, were not. It all smelled—no, reeked—of gender discrimination.

The players were no longer willing to be grateful for simply having the opportunity to play professionally. They were growing tired of waiting for the situation to improve.

> ## "The bottom line is simple. It is wrong for us to be paid and valued less for our work because of our gender."
>
> —Becky Sauerbrunn,
> U.S. defender, 2008–2024

Veteran player Carli Lloyd reminded the public of the team's devotion to the game: "We know the sacrifices we make; it's no different than what men make. We're away from our families. We're away from our friends. We're spending every waking hour dedicating ourselves to this."

The players were done with being treated like second-class citizens.

The lawsuit was huge news from the beginning, immediately making international headlines. The world was looking on, especially female athletes in all sports who had experienced similar discrimination throughout their careers. If the American women could score this win, that could lay the groundwork for equality for everyone else. But if the best team in the world couldn't get equal pay—who could?

Players like Alex Morgan and Megan Rapinoe were already super famous. Alex was known for her speed and goal-scoring prowess on the field, and also for her she-could-be-my-best-friend vibe that landed her magazine covers, big endorsement deals, a kids' book series, and television appearances. Colorful pixie-haired Megan was an incredible asset on the field, and she was known for her outspoken nature and unwavering commitment to her beliefs. After the lawsuit was filed, the players united and utilized their media training to release statements, make talk show appearances, participate in interviews, and publish opinion pieces and essays. They also harnessed the power of their huge social media followings. Thousands immediately showed support online and at matches, letting the federation know that the fans were totally behind the team.

An Ugly Fight

U.S. Soccer responded to the players' lawsuit by denying everything. The federation insisted that the women had actually been paid more than the men during the time period in question.

And that was true—but this was because the women's team had been WAY more successful and played more matches, leading to higher earnings. It wasn't about how much they made in that time period, but the *rate* at which they were paid.

The problem was the women had to work harder and for longer to make the same as the men.

That wasn't fair.

U.S. Soccer had always claimed that the men's compensation was based on "market realities," meaning that men's soccer was generally more moneymaking than women's. But the women's team couldn't see how it could say that when they had generated so much money for the federation—way more than the men's team had.

The federation also argued that the female players had agreed to be paid less in their collective employment contract. Just because the players were now unhappy with it, didn't mean they could break the contract.

But this missed the point again—the players were never even offered the same terms as the men in the first place, which was discrimination. "It was the best deal we could get at the time," Megan Rapinoe explained. The players had also agreed to that deal because they feared if they didn't, the federation would shut down the women's national team.

It was an ugly fight, and one that had started in 2016, when five star players filed a labor complaint against U.S. Soccer with the Equal Employment Opportunity Commission, making similar claims.

But the 2019 lawsuit was a new chapter. This time, the entire national team supported it. The team's senior leaders worked to convince the younger players that they should join the fight too. A lawsuit meant a long battle, a lot of extra media attention, and a big distraction from playing soccer during a World Cup year. And it was just scary being in a legal battle with your employer. The youngest players, Tierna Davidson and Mallory Pugh, were only twenty and twenty-one at the time. They had just fulfilled their dream to play on the national team, and in a World Cup. Was this really their fight? Veteran players like Megan Rapinoe, who had previously boldly stood up for the LGBTQ+ community and was the first U.S. women's soccer player to take a knee during the national anthem to protest racial injustice, took time to talk to the younger players. They wanted to show them that this wasn't just about the salaries of a few players, but about all of them. It was about the generations of girls younger than them, and all female athletes in the U.S. and around the world. A win there was a win for women everywhere and for future generations. It was much bigger than their individual selves. As members of the women's national team, whether they liked it or not, they were role models and had a legacy to leave. Soon enough, the entire team was united.

They would all fight for equality together.

> **We ultimately decided to file this motion for all the little girls around the world who deserve the same respect as the boys. They deserve a voice, and if we as professional athletes don't leverage the voices we have, we are letting them down. We will not let them down.**

—Alex Morgan,
U.S. striker, 2010–2024

With the fans on their side, the players felt even more confident in their position. When the corporate world showed signs of siding with them, it was another huge boost.

- Luna Bar, an energy bar company, pledged a $31,250 bonus to any player who made the World Cup—which represented the difference in World Cup roster bonuses between the men's and women's teams.

- Secret, a women's deodorant company owned by Proctor & Gamble, took out a full-page ad in the *New York Times*, proclaiming its support for the women's team, promising to donate over half a million dollars to the Players Association, and calling on the federation to support "Equal Work. Equal Sweat. Equal Pay."

- One of soccer's most important sponsors, Nike, put out a television ad showing its support for equal pay.

This was the kind of pressure the federation felt most—it depended on those corporate dollars.

While all the public support was supremely important to the players, the team knew the most important thing they needed was a big win at the upcoming World Cup in France. They had to remind the federation and the rest of the world that they were the best of the best. Then, equal pay would be obvious.

Fueled by so much more than their usual desire to win and represent their country, the U.S. women's national team did not disappoint in their eighth World Cup. They put on a spectacular performance throughout the tournament, and when it came to the final against the Netherlands in the *Parc Olympique Lyonnais* in Lyon, France, they got the job done. Senior player Megan Rapinoe and junior player Rose Lavelle both knocked goals into the back of the net, and the U.S. shutout their opponents 2-0.

For the American players, victory was the sweetest it had ever tasted. What made it even sweeter?

In place of the regular words to the classic chant, "U.S.A.! U.S.A.! U.S.A!," the 57,900 fans in the stands slotted in the words "Equal Pay! Equal Pay!"

The American players stood on the field, misty-eyed, looking out at the chanting thousands. They basked not only in the glory of their incredible athletic victory but also in their fans' support for their hard, world-changing fight. It was an unforgettable end to a World Cup.

After the game, the lavender-haired Rapinoe, who had been named player of the game, spoke to the press—but everyone could tell she was really speaking directly to the federation.

"I think we're done with: 'Are we worth it? Should we have equal pay? [Are] the [male and female] markets the same?' Yada, yada. Everyone is done with that. Fans are done with that. The players are done with that . . . What's next? How do we support women's federations and women's programs around the world? . . . It's time to move that conversation forward to the next step."

To celebrate their epic victory, the U.S. women's national team was treated to the traditional ticker tape parade in downtown Manhattan earned by America's best sports teams. The players rode on floats, drank champagne, and waved at their adoring fans, many who had shirts and signs showing their support for their fight.

One float even had a poster that read:
"Parades are cool; equal pay is cooler."

After the parade, the team, their coaches, and representatives of U.S. Soccer gathered on a stage to give speeches. It must have been pretty awkward for Carlos Cordeiro, the then-president of U.S. Soccer. But things got even more awkward for Carlos when fans chanted "equal pay" at the start of his speech, much to the delight of the players. Everyone thought now that the women's team had won again, and it was clear that the public and corporate sponsors were on their side, U.S. Soccer would come to the negotiating table, ready to settle.

But that's not what happened. Instead, U.S. Soccer issued a carefully-worded open letter from Carlos that it blasted to the public two weeks after the World Cup final. Carlos started by complimenting the athletes, saying they were "an inspiration to us all and truly some of the greatest athletes that our nation has ever produced." But then he dug his heels in, stating the women's team was paid differently from the men's because the women's team had agreed to that structure. The two teams' compensation packages were very different and it wasn't an apples-to-apples comparison anyway. The letter added a "fact sheet" where the federation reported: "From 2010 to 2018, U.S. Soccer paid women 34.1 million dollars in salaries and game bonuses and we paid our men 26.4 million dollars."

The players were irate. The federation was making it seem like they were misleading their fans with their claims of unfair pay.

But the reality was the federation was still missing the point: yes, the women's team made more money during that time period, but it was because they won so much more.

The men's team and the women's team weren't paid the same rate and had never even been offered any deal close to that before.

The dispute got even uglier when attempts at arriving at a settlement went nowhere. The parties were just so far apart. The most brutal point came on March 9, 2020 when U.S. Soccer filed a legal brief in court. The brief argued that male players have "more responsibility" and that the men's team "requires a higher level of skill based on speed and strength," citing this as "indisputable science."

U.S. goalkeeper Adrianna Franch warming up in her inside-out jersey during the SheBelieves cup on March 11, 2020.

Excuse me, what?! Female athletes require less skill, effort, and responsibility?

It sounded a lot like that age-old claim that women were biologically inferior to men. Had we gone back in time one hundred years to the days of Dick, Kerr and the fifty-year ban? It was an utterly misogynistic argument.

U.S. Soccer had crossed a line. The backlash was immediate and furious.

The players were completely outraged. In a match against Japan, they defiantly wore their warm-up jerseys inside out to hide the U.S. Soccer crest. Even people who were not soccer fans took to social media to show their disappointment. Corporate sponsors like Volkswagen and Coca-Cola inundated Carlos with expressions of disgust and threatened to pull their sponsorships. In response to the public outrage, the legal brief was retracted. Carlos issued an apology, stating that he hadn't fully read the brief before it was filed, and he announced his resignation. To replace Carlos, Cindy Parlow Cone was instated as the next federation president.

This seemed like good news for the women. Cindy was a player herself, she had been on the famous 1999 U.S. women's national team. She was the first female president of the federation ever. Surely, they would get somewhere with negotiations now.

But on May 1, 2020, with the players and the rest of the world stuck at home as the Covid-19 pandemic was just heating up, something devastating happened. The judge presiding over their case issued a crushing ruling. He agreed with U.S. Soccer that, during the years in question, the women had been paid more than the men. As a result, he did not believe the players had been subjected to pay discrimination. The court dismissed the equal pay claim. Although most of the working conditions claims were allowed to proceed, the heart of the lawsuit had been ripped out, along with all of the hearts of the players.

No one had expected this result. The court had failed to understand the main point, that the rate of pay wasn't the same. It also felt like the teammates were being punished for their wins because the three years mentioned in the lawsuit were when their salaries were at their highest. The players were beyond frustrated and disappointed. But they vowed to appeal the decision.

We knew this wasn't going to be easy, change never is.

–Becky Sauerbrunn,
U.S. defender, 2008–2024

Even though the U.S. women's soccer team had lost in the court of law, they had clearly won in the court of public opinion. And that proved to be the more powerful judge. U.S. Soccer knew they looked bad from the very beginning of this dispute—to players, to fans, to their corporate sponsors, to women generally. Professional athletes like tennis's Serena Williams, and Billie Jean King, Olympic gymnast Aly Raisman, NFL quarterback Aaron Rodgers, and even members of the U.S. men's national team like goalkeeper Tim Howard made their support of the women's team public. So did celebrities like Natalie Portman, Mandy Moore, Eva Longoria, and Regina King.

Even rapper Snoop Dog posted "Pay them ladies, man! Pay them girls what they're worth!" on his social media.

News commentators, politicians, journalists, and important organizations sided with the women. A day after the court ruling, then-presidential candidate Joe Biden vowed, that if he were elected, he would cut funding for the 2026 Men's World Cup unless the federation guaranteed equal pay. The women's team also had the support of the men's national team. U.S. Soccer may have won one battle, but they had lost the war.

A Victory for All Women

Led by former women's national team player, Cindy Parlow Cone, the federation was finally ready to work toward a promise of equal pay. New, fairer employment contracts were to be drawn up. First up, working conditions. The federation agreed to make hotel accommodations, staffing, venues, and travel for the women's team on par with the men's.

But the hardest questions were related to pay, and the biggest sticking point was the World Cup prize money. U.S. Soccer had always argued that the money came from FIFA, not from them, and it wasn't the federation's fault that FIFA paid out the men's and women's portion unequally. The players found this unconvincing. Yes, FIFA is the one who assigned the amount of prize money for the men's and women's cups, but it paid the money directly to the national federations. U.S. Soccer was the one who actually sent the checks to its players. If the federation ultimately controlled that money, couldn't it pool it, then dole it out equally? For that to happen, the men's national team had to cooperate. In the name of progress—plus a healthy fear of public backlash, the potential for new kinds of financial benefits, and with the security of their hefty club team salaries—the men's team got on board. That was the final piece of the puzzle.

- Now, the men's and women's teams had the same contract, on equal terms, and were paid the same, dollar-for-dollar.

- There were increased rates for matches played and the matches won, and increased rates for public appearances.

- The World Cup prize money was now pooled and divided equally.

- The men's and women's players also had an equal share of the money brought in by broadcasts, partners, and sponsorships, plus ticket sales for U.S. Soccer-controlled games.

Hall of Fame
Megan Rapinoe

For Megan Rapinoe, being a professional athlete was never just about soccer—it was about much more. As a winger for the national team, she proudly came out as gay and became a vocal advocate for the LGBTQ+ community, especially athletes. Her natural confidence helped her wow on the pitch and also speak out against injustice. In the face of many critics, "Pinoe," as she's called by her teammates, began kneeling during the national anthem to protest racial inequality. She also became the face of the equal pay fight, publicly leading the battle against U.S. Soccer. She has been vocal about her support for trans athletes. As a player, Megan asked herself: "Who do you want to be? What kind of person do you want to be for yourself, but also in the larger context of the country and in the world?" She'll be remembered both for her larger-than-life, vocal personality and the awesome soccer skills which helped her win two World Cups, two Olympic gold medals, and numerous accolades. In 2022, Megan was awarded the Presidential Medal of Freedom. Post-retirement, Megan continues to use her voice as an activist.

This was the first time in soccer history that every single aspect of the gender pay gap was addressed, including World Cup prize money.

On top of all of these changes, the federation also agreed to pay the twenty-eight players named in the lawsuit a total of 24 million dollars in back pay. While it wasn't the 67 million dollars they had asked for, it was still an enormous sum, and the changes the players made in achieving fair pay for the future was the real win. The cherry on top of this remarkable deal? The federation also agreed to pay 2 million dollars to a charitable fund supporting women's and girls' soccer. With this new agreement, U.S. Soccer was hoping to heal its image in the public and was now ready for a new chapter in their relationship with their female players—one where they were on the same winning team.

The players had done it. They could now declare victory. They had achieved equal pay—for themselves, and for generations of women to come.

> **This is going to be one of those incredible moments that we look back on and say the game changed forever, U.S. Soccer changed forever, and the landscape of soccer in this country and in the world changed forever.**
>
> —Megan Rapinoe,
> U.S. midfielder, 2006–2023

The effect of the U.S. women's national team's bold and inspiring actions rippled across the world. Australia, Norway, New Zealand, Brazil, Ireland, Spain, the Netherlands, and Canada's teams each struck their own fair pay deals, some even before the U.S. had finalized its own. Some of these deals involved equal percentages of the World Cup money and not equal dollar-for-dollar portions, but, regardless, these female footballers had reason to celebrate.

Outside of soccer, the U.S. women's victory emboldened female athletes of all sports to fight for better working conditions and compensation. The team even inspired a federal law to be passed. In January 2023, President Joe Biden signed the Equal Pay for Team USA Act, ensuring that all American athletes, regardless of their gender, will receive equal compensation when they represent the U.S. in global tournaments like the World Cup, the Olympics, and the Paralympics. When it came to world-class athletes competing in world-class tournaments, equal pay was now the law of the land in America.

Global Game: Nigeria

In 2004, after winning the African Women's Championship, the Nigerian women's national team grabbed their hard-earned trophy and locked themselves in a hotel in protest for unpaid winnings. This standoff made headlines across Africa and beyond. It was embarrassing for Nigeria's football federation and for the whole country. The girls' risk paid off, and they were finally paid. When they returned home to Nigeria, they were welcomed with a party at the president's house and received bonus money and academic scholarships, making it a double victory for this bold team.

Goalkeeper Mary Earps and forward Lauren James share a moment of solidarity on the pitch.

Global Game: England

England is where women's football got its start, but it's also the country responsible for the lowest point in the sport's history—the fifty-year ban. After the ban was lifted in 1971, progress was slow in attracting English players and fans. Even after the national team was well established and women's football had become popular around the world, most of England still seemed uninterested in women's football.

That all changed in the summer of 2022, when Lioness fever took hold of the country. The UEFA European Women's Championship—the Euros—took place in England. The host nation's team, led by Beth Mead and Leah Williamson, put in a spectacular performance, ultimately winning the whole tournament. This victory marked England's first major international sports title in 56 years—something no men's team had been able to accomplish. Having captured the attention of their nation, the Lionesses used their newfound fame to push for the growth of their sport, demanding equal access to football for girls in school. Since their big win, there's been a big bump in youth players, a bigger fandom that regularly fills stadiums, and more and more women cropping up in all facets of the sport, including coaching, staffing, and broadcasting. There's no looking back for the Lionesses, with new, young stars like Lauren James and Mary Earps being hailed as the best in the world. The country that helped launch women's football can now boast one of the most supportive and developed football programs for women and girls in the world.

13

Defeating Abuse

*I*magine it's the 1990s, and you're a young girl living in a working-class neighborhood in Madrid, Spain. Your grandfather was a professional footballer—a goalkeeper. You love the game too. Your dad takes you to play in the park and spends hours training you. You spend your early years playing on boys' teams. You're good. Very good. You dream of playing for a professional women's team. And then at fourteen, you get that chance when you play for Atlético Madrid, the same club your grandfather played for. You know you're gay but don't feel like you can be open about it with your parents. With your teammates though, you find it easy to be yourself.

Now imagine that you've become so impressive that you get called up to play for Spain's national team. "La Roja," as this red-kitted squad is lovingly called, is better than it's ever been. And you are its all-time top goal scorer. Your biggest dream is to go to the World Cup—and win it. In 2023, you start to think that dream might actually come true when Spain qualifies for the tournament. The team makes it out of the round of sixteen, into the quarterfinals, then the semi-finals, and finally, you are in the final match against England. You help La Roja outplay the English "Lionesses" and beat them 1-0. Spain is officially the best team in the world. This is everything you've ever dreamed of. It's the highest high you've ever felt in your entire athletic career. Now imagine it's time for you to collect your medal and shake hands with football's bigwigs. When you reach your federation's president, you expect a happy handshake. But something else happens. Instead, he grabs your head and forces a kiss upon your mouth. Your insides recoil. Did that really just happen? You've been waiting your whole life for this triumph and had worked so hard for it—but now, your victory is forever marred by a man's decision.

This is the story of one of Spain's star players, forward Jenni Hermoso. On August 20, 2023, at the World Cup final in the Stadium Australia in Sydney, Jenni's life changed—but not in the way she expected. It was an impressive match, where *La Roja* showed off its technical skill and its ability to command the field. Jenni was disappointed when she missed a penalty kick, but a pretty goal from Olga Carmona gave Spain the lead they deserved over the Lionesses.

When the final whistle blew, Jenni and her teammates whooped, wept, hugged, and dogpiled. To them, this was everything.

Shortly after, it was time to receive their championship medals. Spain's Queen Letizia, her sixteen-year-old daughter, Princess Sofía, members of FIFA and the Royal Spanish Football Federation (known as RFEF), including its president Luis Rubiales were waiting on a podium to bestow the medals and congratulate them.

As the players made their way down the podium one by one, Rubiales enthusiastically congratulated the women, planted kisses on their cheeks and necks, and lifted some women off the ground. When it was Jenni's turn to receive her congratulations from Rubiales, in front of an audience of millions, he grabbed the back of her head with both hands and kissed her on the lips without any notice or permission. Both Jenni and Rubiales continued on with the procession from there.

Spain's players celebrate after becoming FIFA World Cup champions.

Right after the ceremony, while on an Instagram livestream, Jenni and her teammates watched footage of the kiss from the locker room. Jenni, known for her good nature and wit, was not laughing now. She reacted: "I didn't like it." And neither did viewers. Right away, people's discomfort with the interaction was voiced.

Everyone should have been talking about how Spain had effortlessly beat England. But instead, people were becoming fixated on the inappropriate move by the federation president.

Rubiales had to explain himself almost immediately, during a post-match interview with a Spanish radio station in which he claimed it was a "peck between two friends celebrating something."

Post-match, the public was still tittering. People on social media and members of the press expressed how unacceptable they thought Rubiales' behavior was. *This was assault*, many declared. Realizing that this wasn't going to just go away, Rubiales and other members of the RFEF approached Jenni on the team bus, and again on the plane ride home from Sydney, insisting that she sign a statement saying the kiss was consensual. Jenni battled tears because she didn't want to affect her team's celebratory mood. Despite the intense pressure from her powerful employers, she wasn't having it. She continued to refuse. No one could have guessed that the following days would be the wildest all of Spanish football had ever seen.

One day after the historic win, the RFEF released a statement, quoting Jenni. "It was a mutual, totally spontaneous gesture because of the huge joy of winning a World Cup. The 'presi' [Rubiales] and I have a great relationship . . . It was a natural gesture of affection and gratitude."

There was only one problem with the statement. Jenni had never said anything of the sort. It seemed that the RFEF had made it all up.

"I didn't say a single word of that text," she said later. "I felt coerced again."

Rubiales must have sensed that the public expected an apology, so on the same day that the RFEF released the likely fabricated statement, he put out a video statement saying his actions were "normal, natural and not at all with any bad faith." He continued by saying, "Of course, if there are people who felt hurt by this, I need to apologize."

In other words, it was a non-apology.

Unsurprisingly, this didn't go over well with a lot of the public. Both the global footballers' union and the Spanish women's players' union called for Rubiales to be punished for his actions. FIFA launched an investigation into him for violating "basic rules of decent conduct." Many were calling for Rubiales to resign. The blowback wasn't limited to Spain—millions around the world had been watching and the outcry was now global.

But not everyone was outraged by Rubiales. *What's the big deal?* some expressed. *This is silliness*, some mainstream Spanish media outlets declared. Spain was a country known for its history of "machismo," a culture of deeply held masculine pride where manliness was valued above all. To some, it should be socially acceptable for a man to kiss a woman who works with him in a moment of celebration. Even though Spain had evolved over the years, it still had a long way to go. And it was clear that the world of football was still steeped in that old-school chauvinistic culture.

While all of this discourse was happening, Jenni and her teammates were partying on the island of Ibiza, basking in the sun and celebrating their win. But even there, she wasn't safe from pressure from the Spanish soccer world. It was revealed later that the RFEF sent executives to hound Jenni into saying that the kiss was consensual. But with the support of her teammates, Jenni stood strong.

You would think when much of the world was condemning your actions, you may start to see the error of your ways. But not Rubiales. On August 25th, just five days after the final, he stood in front of an assembly of members of the RFEF and declared defiantly: "I'm not going to resign, I'm not going to resign, I'm not going to resign, I'm not going to resign." He also told a new version of the events: Jenni lifted *him* up and he asked if he could kiss her and she had agreed—the kiss was consensual. He even brought his daughters into this mess by claiming, "The kiss was the same I could give one of my daughters." He said he was a victim of "false feminism" and that his character was being assassinated. He vowed to "fight to the end," and promised to pursue legal action against anyone who called the kiss "assault." This was the opposite of an apology—it was a declaration of war. Against Jenni, female footballers, and anyone who took their side. He received a standing ovation from the practically all-male audience that included *La Roja* coach Jorge Vilda and the men's team head coach, Luis De la Fuente. Of course, Rubiales' fiery antics made international headlines, infuriating many.

The Spanish players had had enough of this open misogyny. What Rubiales had done to Jenni was wrong, and his behavior afterward was even worse. It wasn't just Rubiales who was a villain, but the whole Spanish football system seemed to be against women. What could they do to fight this?

They did the most powerful thing they could think of—band together as one.

A Full-on Revolution

Hours after Rubiales' unrepentant speech, eighty-one Spanish female footballers, including all twenty-three members of the World Cup-winning squad, refused to play for the national team until Rubiales was fired or resigned. He was "violating the dignity of women."

The world also heard directly—and for real—from Jenni for the first time. She made her truth clear:

"I want to clarify that, as seen in the images, at no time did I consent to the kiss that he gave me and of course, in no case did I seek to lift up the president. I will not tolerate that my word is doubted, much less have words that I have not said invented."

Support for Jenni and her teammates poured in, from Spain and around the world. Players on the men's national team stood by their female counterparts, with Iker Casillas, Spain's goalkeeper, tweeting:

 Iker Casillas
@Spain Goalkeeper, 2000-2016

What an embarrassment. We should have spent the last five days talking about our women players, about the joy they gave us all! About how proud we are that they gave us a title that we didn't have in women's soccer, instead . . .

#SeAcabó ¡NO ESTÁS SOLA!

"*Se Acabó*" ("It's Over") became the team's rally cry against sexism and mistreatment. In solidarity, male and female athletes around the world put the phrase on jerseys and on tape around their wrists. Soon, "*se acabó*" took on a whole new meaning—women across Spain started speaking out against the sexist and misogynist behavior they had endured. Spain had been mostly unaffected by America's #MeToo movement six years prior, but now its women were ready to speak up, no longer afraid of the consequences of revealing abuse.

Jenni and her teammates had started a full-on revolution.

The world was angry, FIFA was angry, professional athletes around the world were expressing their disapproval, and the entire pool of female football talent in Spain was on strike. But the RFEF reacted by doubling down on their support for their president.

Finally, just eight days after Spain won the Women's World Cup, with an enormous amount of pressure mounting, members of the RFEF realized that they had nothing to gain by continuing to support Rubiales. It announced that Spain's soccer federation had fired its president.

Role Models

Jenni and the rest of Spain's female footballers were again triumphant. But their fight against sexism in football wasn't over. Especially for Jenni. Not only did she have to relive her experiences in court during the legal phase of this sorry incident, but she was left off the roster after the team's first match after the tournament. The only thing that heartened her was watching the match on television and spotting "*se acabó*" written on the wrists of her teammates.

Jenni Hermoso at the 2023 FIFA Women's World Cup.

Despite everything, Jenni had plenty to be excited about. She was given a hero's welcome back to her club team, *Pachuca*, greeted by a giant banner held up by fans emblazoned with her image. She was able to regain her spot on the national team. She was hired as co-presenter for Spain's New Year's Eve celebrations, was named *The Guardian*'s Footballer of the Year, and was one of *Time* Magazine's Most Influential People of 2024. To many in Spain and around the globe, Jenni was a role model. Jenni didn't mean to become an advocate for women's rights. She believed her purpose was soccer—but soccer led her to a new purpose. Although the assault and its aftermath were horrible to deal with, in the end, "I feel strong and I am not defeated," Jenni told reporters.

Because of Jenni's bravery, the world awoke to an ugly truth about women's soccer, and women's sports in general. Despite the many gains they had made, female athletes continued to suffer mistreatment. By standing up to Rubiales and their powerful federation, Jenni and her teammates showed that justice could be served, that change was necessary, and they made it easier for countless others to speak out against abuse.

These female footballers proved that when women speak up, change can be made.

14

The Future is Female

When women first gathered together to play organized soccer, it was considered a spectacle. To the people curiously watching, these matches were acts of theater or comedy or even the actual circus.

But to the players, they were acts of defiance, athleticism, and freedom.

If you told those first Scottish and English players from 1881, who were chased off the pitch, that soccer would eventually become the most popular women's sport, played by millions of girls and women around the world, would they believe you?

And would Nettie Honeyball, who scandalized Britain by having the British Ladies Football Club play soccer in bloomers, be surprised to see professional female footballers sporting state-of-the-art kits just like men?

Would the Dick, Kerr Ladies, banned from stepping foot in men's venues, be delighted to know that we now live in a world where women's football sells out huge stadiums?

And are those early national team players from the eighties and nineties, who had to stay in roach motels and play for free, proud that many female national teams are now paid equally to men's teams?

In 150 years, women's soccer has come so far. Not just in big ways but in many small ways too. For players, more attention is being paid to what exactly it takes to support a female athlete. For example, there's been a push to dedicate more scientific research to improve and tailor gear and training to female bodies. Team doctors figured out that adding the tracking of menstrual periods as a data point helped maintain the health and strength of their athletes. More benefits are offered than ever before, including mental health support and childcare, providing supportive tools so that players can balance family and a pro athlete career. The athletes play in better conditions—and have their own stadiums. In 2024, CPKC Stadium in Kansas City, Missouri became the very first stadium in the world dedicated to a women's sports team. More policies have been put in place to protect female players from mistreatment. And the sport is more welcoming than ever, ushering in players from all walks of life, backgrounds, and identities who find joy in the game. In 2023, the *Washington Post* declared in a headline:

> **"This is the gayest World Cup ever (and no one's batting an eyelid)."**

Nearly 100 World Cup players on twenty-two of the thirty teams competing identified as LGBTQ, including major stars.

The 2024 Olympic Games hosted one of the most diverse women's football tournaments ever. The U.S. won gold with the help of a record-breaking eight Black players on its team, including its superstar trio of strikers, Mallory Pugh Swanson, Trinity Rodman, and Sophia Smith.

Beyond the players, there are more female owners, coaches, referees, staff, broadcasters, and journalists—not just limited to women's football, they are being

hired for pro men's teams too. The football commentating world used to be a "boy's club," but now you regularly see female commentators like former Lioness Alex Scott and former U.S. player Julie Foudy on television screens during women's and men's matches.

When it comes to the fans, there are more dedicated spaces for female sports enthusiasts, including *The Sports Bra* in Portland, Oregon and *Rough and Tumble* in Seattle, Washington that prioritize women's sports on their screens. Stadiums in Turkey and Brazil have even sponsored women's nights, where entire stadiums are filled with only female fans. While there is more room to grow and stubborn stereotypes and prejudices left to defeat, all of these changes show so much respect for the sport and its athletes, promising an incredible future.

It's an amazing time to be a women's soccer fan and player. It's also amazing to look back and see how we got here. From the beginning of soccer's history, women were always there. Although many people were just not paying attention or neglecting to record it in history books, women were running and kicking and scoring goals.

Like magnets, they were drawn to the sport and found a way to play, even when it was hard. They battled through different eras of obstacles. At first, it was: *women shouldn't play at all.* Then, it was: *women can't play well enough.* Then: *women shouldn't be paid to play.* And *women's teams aren't equal to men's teams.*

Through it all, women persisted and kept playing, setting new goals to achieve.

Every single time, they fought for what they thought they deserved—and got it. And in the process, inspired women and girls around the world. The story of women's soccer is one of victory, where a love of the game has always won out, and where women are always the champions.

A beautiful game, indeed.

⬡ ⬡ ⬡

Acknowledgments

What a joy and honor it was to research and relay the stories of these incredible women in this special sport that has always meant so much to me. Writing this book would not have been possible without the support and work of others.

I have to first thank my biggest cheerleader and advocate, my dear friend and literary agent (in that order), Lilly Ghahremani. She was the first to believe that I was a writer as much as I was an agent and an editor. She also kept circling back on the idea of this book—even when I was initially too scared to write about a topic I cared so much about. She's an exceptional agent, great at every aspect of the job. I feel so lucky to have her as my champion. My gratitude also extends to Stefanie Sanchez Van Borstel, who captains the ship at Full Circle Literary, an exceptional place to be a client.

I relied on the important work of many academics, journalists, authors and documentarians to relay this history. Women's history has so often gone unrecorded and these individuals have done the difficult, important work of digging up amazing stories and details. Some had to dig really hard! Just to name a few: Jean Williams, Gail Newsham, Patrick Brennan, Brenda Elsey, Joshua Nadal, Andrew Das, Caitlin Murray, Chuka Onwumechili, Rachel Ramsay, and James Erskine. I look forward to the future work of others, including those who uncover the yet unknown early histories of women's football in countries like my father's Peru.

It takes a whole team of publishing professionals to create a book, and I'm so grateful for mine at Holler and Quarto. A very special thank you to Debbie Foy, who understood the power of this book right away and guided me to give it the global scope the subject deserved. And to Hollie Cayzer, for her kindness and sharp editorial eye. The enthusiasm you both shared for this book helped me see it through to the end. Michelle Brackenborough, your talent elevated this book beyond my biggest expectations.

Thank you to the friends who pitched in in various ways: Erin Bruno, Caitlin Shadek, Jessica McSherry, Benjamin Stauber, Ari Segal, Barbara Middleton, and Jim Morrison.

The support of these special cheerleaders in my life was deeply felt during the writing of this book: Gina Chung, Cindy Uh, Adria Goetz, Mondi Basmenji, Cory Black, Alexandra

Workman, Juliana Finegan, Allison Paul, Jessie Rosen, and Tiphaine Croville. Much love to my Seattle critique group: Rob Albanese, Vashti Verbowski, Ruthie Nicklaus, Kirstin Larson, and Kirsti Ringger. A special squeeze to my former writing community in Singapore who continue to root for me from a world away: Namita Moolani Mehra, Pippa Chorley, Leila Boukarim, Charles Santoso, Evelyn Wong, Srividhya Venkat, Katherine Wallace, Barbara Moxham, and David Liew. And appreciation for my former clients, whose talent inspired me and helped me get here.

I'm grateful every day for the endless support of my best friend, my sister, Claudia. I so appreciate my brothers Jean-Louis and Sebastian, football experts in their own right, who answered my many texts of random questions. And my brother Fabrizio, who always remembers to ask me about my work. Hugs to my siblings' partners, Ivy, Liz, and Neil. My parents, Agnes and Hugo, have always stood by me as I took the winding way on my career journey—that has meant the world to me.

I have to acknowledge my former teammates who happen to also be some of my best friends in the world: Lauren Mendelsohn, Caitlin Shadek, Allison DiClemente, Erin Bruno, and Blair Dver. I feel so lucky that soccer brought us all together as kids. It's very fitting that I found out this book was a go while we were all sitting in a pool together in Mexico.

Without the aid of Julia Carrillo-Bustamante, finishing this book simply wouldn't have been possible. Thank you for the love and dedicated care you have given my daughters.

To my daughters, Azalea and Samantha, I have this to say: *Iceland's little yaks swim mightily*. And to my husband, Michael, who has never flinched a single time I concocted a wild plan, including to become an author. I love and appreciate you beyond words.

And finally, a bighearted thank you to all of the women's soccer players who have influenced me, before, during, and after writing this book. You amaze me, you empower me, you inspire me. I have a very special spot in my heart for the 99ers, who made me feel my own power for one of the first times in my life. I know I'm not alone in that. I hope I did all of these amazing women justice with this project. Cheers.

References

Abnos, Alexander. "The 10 Most Significant Goals in U.S. Soccer History: 4: Start of Something Big." *Sports Illustrated.* si.com/specials/longform/soccer-goals/goal4.html

Barbara Middleton. (1970s College Soccer Player, Retired School Librarian), in discussion with the author, March 19, 2024.

Bell, Jack. "America Offers Opportunities for Foreign Soccer Players." *New York Times.* Sept. 2, 2002. archive.nytimes.com/www.nytimes.com/library/sports/soccer/090200soc-women.html

Blumenthal, Karen. *Let Me Play: The Story of Title IX: The Law that Changed the Future of Girls in America.* New York, New York: Atheneum Books for Young Readers, 2023.

Bonesteel, Matt. "A Timeline of the U.S. Women's Soccer Team's Equal Pay Dispute with U.S. Soccer." *Washington Post.* Feb. 22, 2022. washingtonpost.com/sports/2022/02/22/uswnt-pay-lawsuit-timeline/?utm_source=pocket_saves

Boschert, Sherry. *37 Words: Title IX and Fifty Years of Fighting Sex Discrimination.* New York, New York: The New Pres, 2022.

Brennan, Patrick. "British Ladies Football Club." Donmouth. donmouth.co.uk/womens_football/blfc.html

Brennan, Patrick. "The Dick, Kerr Ladies' FC." Donmouth. donmouth.co.uk/womens_football/dick_kerr.html

Brennan, Patrick. "'England' v. 'Scotland' – 1881: First Attempt to Establish Women's Soccer Disrupted by Soccer Hooligans." Donmouth. donmouth.co.uk/womens_football/1881.html

Brewster, Claire and Keith Brewster. "'A Lesson in Football Wisdom?' Coverage of the Unofficial Women's World Cup of 1971 in the Mexican Press." *Sport in History* 39, no. 2 (March 28, 2019): 147–165. doi.org/10.1080/17460263.2019.1592015

Chaundler, Rachel. "Spanish Soccer Official Apologizes, Sort of, for Kissing World Cup Winner." *New York Times.* Aug. 21, 2023. nytimes.com/2023/08/21/world/europe/spain-soccer-kiss-rubiales-hermoso-apology.html

Civin, Todd. "Women's Pro Soccer is All A Twitter." *Bleacher Report.* May 3, 2009. bleacherreport.com/articles/167254-womens-pro-soccer-is-all-a-twitter

Cordeiro, Carlos (@CACSoccer). "My letter and fact sheet to our soccer community about the @USWNT lawsuit. We're committed to doing right by our women's players, and I'm optimistic we can get this done." Twitter, July 29, 2019. x.com/CACSoccer/status/1155951850685755394

Corti, Andrea Nix, and Sean Fine, dirs. *LFG.* HBO Max, June 24, 2021.

Das, Andrew. "The U.S. Women Won, the Men Lost, and the Equal Pay Fight that Tied Them Together Again." *New York Times.* July 10, 2019. nytimes.com/2019/07/10/sports/soccer/soccer-parade.html?searchResultPosition=34&utm_source=pocket_reader

Doyle, Paul. "Women's World Cup Game-Changing Moments No 2: Denmark in 1971." *The Guardian.* June 13, 2019. theguardian.com/football/2019/jun/13/womens-world-cup-game-changing-moments-no-2-denmark-in-1971

Dunn, Carrie. *'Unsuitable for Females': The Rise of the Lionesses and Women's Football in England.* Rev ed. Edinburgh, United Kingdom: Arena Sport, 2022.

Elsey, Brenda and Joshua Nadel. *Futbolera: A History of Women and Sports in Latin America.* Austin, Texas: University of Texas Press, 2019.

FIFA. "Raising Their Game: Blazing the Way in 1991." *YouTube video.* 8:42. June 12, 2012. youtube.com/watch?v=83Q4PSuR34c

Hall, Matthew. "Copa 71: When 112,500 Fans Packed Out the Unofficial Women's World Cup Final." *The Guardian.* Sept 8, 2023. bbc.com/news/business-46149887?utm_source=pocket_reader

Goff, Steven. "NWSL Enjoying a World Cup Bump, But Sustainability is Next Step." *Washington Post.* July 28, 2019. washingtonpost.com/sports/2019/07/28/nwsl-enjoying-world-cup-bump-sustainability-is-next-step/

Goldblatt, David. *The Ball is Round: A Global History of Soccer.* New York, New York: Riverhead Books, 2008.

Goldman, Rob. *The Sisterhood: The 99ers and the Rise of U.S. Women's Soccer.* Lincoln, Nebraska: University of Nebraska Press, 2021.

Goodman, Al and Claudia Rebaza. "Jennifer Hermoso's Lawyer Reiterates that Kiss by Luis Rubiales was Non-Consensual as Former Soccer Boss Handed Restraining Order." CNN. Sept. 15, 2023. cnn.com/2023/09/15/football/jennifer-hermoso-luis-rubiales-court-lawyer-spt-intl/index.html

Goodman, Lizzy. "The Best Women's Soccer Team in the World Fights for Equal Pay." *New York Times Magazine.* June 10, 2019. nytimes.com/2019/06/10/magazine/womens-soccer-inequality-pay.html?searchResultPosition=36&utm_source=pocket_reader

Grainey, Timothy F. *Beyond Bend It Like Beckham: The Global Phenomenon of Women's Soccer.* Lincoln, Nebraska: University of Nebraska Press, 2012.

Hong, Fan, ed. *Soccer, Women, Sexual Liberation: Kicking Off a New Era.* London, United Kingdom: Routledge, 2003.

Jacobs, Barbara. *The Dick, Kerr's Ladies.* London, United Kingdom: Robinson Publishing, 2004.

Kassam, Ashifa. "'Social Assassination': Defiant Rubiales Refuses to Resign Over World Cup Kiss." *The Guardian.* Aug 25, 2023. theguardian.com/football/2023/aug/25/defiant-rubiales-bemoans-social-assassination-and-vows-to-stay-as-spanish-fa-head

Kirby, Paul. "Spain's Hermoso Says Image Tarnished by Rubiales World Cup Kiss." BBC. Oct. 10, 2023. bbc.com/news/world-europe-67063403

Laverty, Rich. "The Inside, Untold Stories of the 1991 Women's World Cup." Women's Football Chronicles. July 19, 2023. richlaverty.substack.com/p/the-inside-untold-stories-of-the

Lisi, Clemente A. *The U.S. Women's Soccer Team: An American Success Story*. 2d. ed. Lanham, Maryland: Scarecrow Press. 2013.

Longman, Jere. "All is Ready and the Stands are Full." *New York Times*. June 19, 1999. archive.nytimes.com/www.nytimes.com/library/sports/soccer/061999soc-wc-opener.html

Longman, Jere. *The Girls of Summer: The U.S. Women's Soccer Team and How it Changed the World*. New York, New York: Harper Perennial, 2001.

Leyden, Erin, dir., *The 99ers*. ESPN Films, July 2, 2013.

Markovits, Andrei S. *Women in American Soccer and European Football: Different Roads to Shared Glory*. Nantucket, Massachusetts: Dickinson-Moses Press, 2023.

Meschke, Jacob. "Overlooked No More: Lily Parr, Dominant British Soccer Player." *New York Times*. July 21, 2023. nytimes.com/2023/07/21/obituaries/lily-parr-overlooked.html

Morgan, Alex. "I Won't Back Down Until There's Equal Pay for Equal Play." Cosmopolitan. April 12, 2016. cosmopolitan.com/politics/a56699/alex-morgan-equal-pay-soccer/

Murray, Caitlin. *The National Team: The Inside Story of the Women Who Changed Soccer*. New York, New York: Abrams Press, 2019

Newsham, Gail J., *In a League of Their Own: The Dick, Kerr Ladies 1917-1965*. Rev. ed. Rogersthorpe, Northhampton, United Kingdom: Gail J. Newsham/Paragon Publishing, 2014.

Nusbaum, Eric. "The Epic, Forgotten 1971 Women's World Cup." *Sports Stories*. Jan. 22, 2020. sportsstories.substack.com/p/the-epic-forgotten-1971-womens-world?utm_source=pocket_reader

Onwumechili, Chuka. *Women's Football in Africa*. London, United Kingdom: Routledge, 2024.

Oxenham, Gwendolyn. *Pride of a Nation: A Celebration of the U.S. Women's National Soccer Team*. New York, New York: Ten Speed Press, 2022.

Pathak, Manasi. "Jenni Hermoso Says She Received Threats After Rubiales' Unsolicited Kiss." *Forbes*. Nov. 7, 2023. forbes.com/sites/manasipathak-1/2023/11/07/jenni-hermoso-says-she-received-threats-after-luis-rubiales-unsolicited-kiss/

Pieper, Lindsay. "The Beleaguered History of the Women's World Cup." Sport in American History. July 2, 2015. ussporthistory.com/2015/07/02/the-beleaguered-history-of-the-womens-world-cup/

Rabeux, Thibault. Trans. Drew Lilly. *Women's Soccer: The Official History of the Unofficial World Cups*. Self-published, 2019.

Rampling, Ali. "Jenni Hermoso and Luis Rubiales: A timeline of what happened after Spain's World Cup win." *The Athletic*. Aug. 26, 2023. nytimes.com/athletic/4807705/2023/08/26/jenni-hermoso-luis-rubiales-timeline/

Rampling, Ali. "Luis Rubiales provisionally suspended by FIFA for Jenni Hermoso kiss." *The Athletic*. Aug. 26, 2023. nytimes.com/athletic/4807509/2023/08/26/luis-rubiales-suspended-fifa/

Ramsay, Rachel and James Erskine, dirs. *Copa 71*. Dogwoof, Sept. 7, 2023.

Rios, Carmen. "What Patsy Mink Made Possible: Title IX at 50." National Women's History Museum. Aug. 26, 2022. womenshistory.org/articles/what-patsy-mink-made-possible-title-ix-50

Schulman, Ken. "'Let's Move On This': The '99 U.S. Women's National Team's Fight for Equality." Only a Game. WBUR Radio. June 7, 2019. wbur.org/onlyagame/2019/06/07/lilly-foudy-lockout-world-cup-team-usa

Steafel, Eleanor. "The Forgotten First Lionesses Who Won the Hearts of Mexico." *The Sunday Telegraph*. June 9, 2019. pressreader.com/uk/the-sunday-telegraph/20190609/282011853861571

Straus, Brian. "Women's Pro Soccer League Forced to Fold." *Washington Post*. Sept. 16, 2003. washingtonpost.com/archive/politics/2003/09/16/womens-pro-soccer-league-forced-to-fold/d3e974bd-62a9-4e41-ad11-ab524c2961e3/

Straus, Brian. "WUSA: Following the Phenomenal Success of the 1999 Women's World Cup the First Women's Professional Soccer League was Formed Around the Core of the US National Team But to Succeed it Will Have to Be More than Mia Vs. Brandy." *Washington Post*. April 13, 2001. washingtonpost.com/archive/sports/2001/04/13/wusa-following-the-phenomenal-success-of-the-1999-womens-world-cup-the-first-womens-professional-soccer-league-was-formed-around-the-core-of-the-us-national-team-but-to-succeed-it-will-have-to-be-more-than-mia-vs-brandi/fcbd430e-7faa-45bf-b656-81d8dbaa570b/

Sauerbrunn, Becky (@beckysauerbrunn). "If you know this team at all you know we have a lot of fight left in us. We knew this wasn't going to be easy, change never is." *Twitter*, May 1, 2020. x.com/beckysauerbrunn/status/1256371988999766017?lang=en

Tate, Tim. *Girls with Balls: The Secret History of Women's Football*. London, United Kingdom: John Blake Books, 2013.

Thompson, Alyssa. "A night to remember." *Instagram*, May 15, 2023, @alyssthomp. instagram.com/alyssthomp/p/CsRxK2aScdv/?img_index=2

U.S. Code. Title IX, Education Amendments of 1972. Public Law No. 92-318, 20 U.S.C. §§ 16981-1688 (1972).

"U.S. Women's National Soccer Team Members Wary About Launch of New Pro League." *Sports Business Journal.* Dec. 17, 2012. sportsbusinessjournal.com/Daily/Issues/2012/12/17/Leagues-and-Governing-Bodies/Womens-Soccer.aspx

USWNT Classics. "Snoop Dogg on WSWNT: "Pay 'Dem Ladies What They Worth Over the Sorry Ass Men!" *YouTube video.* July 8. 2019. youtube.com/watch?v=UFlDgtwAwP0

Vertinsky, Patricia. *The Eternally Wounded Woman: Women, Doctors, and Exercise in the Late Nineteenth Century.* Urbana and Chicago, Illinois: University of Illinois Press, 1994.

Vinall, Frances. "This is the gayest World Cup ever (and no one's batting an eyelid.)" *Washington Post.* Aug. 16, 2023. washingtonpost.com/sports/2023/08/16/womens-world-cup-gay-players-lgbt/

Wahl, Grant. "How the Women's World Cup and USWNT were Built from Scratch." *Sports Illustrated.* June 6, 2019. si.com/soccer/2019/06/06/first-womens-world-cup-1991-uswnt-usa-sepp-blatter

Williams, Jean. *A Beautiful Game: International Perspectives on Women's Football.* Oxford, United Kingdom: Berg Publishers, 2007.

Williams, Jean. *The History of Women's Football.* Yorkshire, United Kingdom: Pen & Sword Books Ltd., 2021.

Wilson, Joseph. "Spain Soccer Head Won't Resign for Kissing Player at World Cup. Team Won't Play Until He Does." Associated Press, Aug. 25, 2023. apnews.com/article/rubiales-spanish-soccer-federation-president-kiss-womens-world-cup-3be367f0de6fbf1984e4885df0dcb00c

WoSoNostalgia. "Highlights of the first Women's World Cup in China 1991." *YouTube video.* 53:41. Nov. 30, 2016. youtube.com/watch?v=DtpYkNGulrQ

Wrack, Suzanne. "How the FA Banned Women's Football in 1921 and Tried to Justify It." *The Guardian.* June 13, 2022. theguardian.com/football/2022/jun/13/how-the-fa-banned-womens-football-in-1921-and-tried-to-justify-it

Wrack, Suzanne. *A Women's Game: The Rise, Fall, and Rise Again of Women's Soccer.* Chicago, Illinois: Triumph Books, 2022.

Yohn Voker. "WUSA: The History in the Making." *YouTube video.* 38:52. July 18, 2016. youtube.com/watch?v=pjaHDRdb_Kg

Zirin, Dave. "U.S. Women's Soccer and the Fight for Equal Pay." *The Nation.* March 18, 2019. thenation.com/article/archive/us-womens-soccer-pay-equity-lawsuit/

Picture Credits

Other Credits